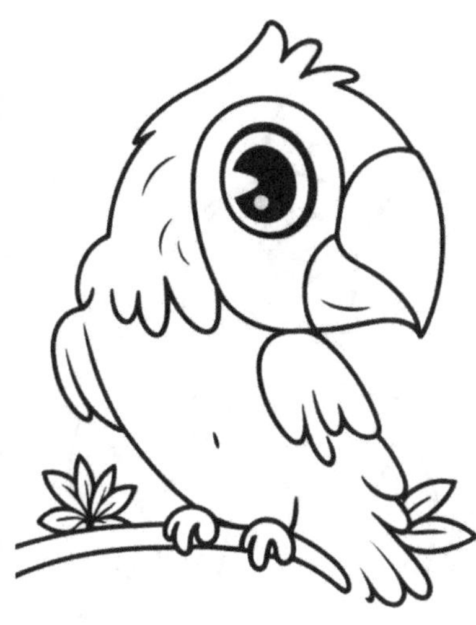 

For all the creative and curious children out there, who bring color and joy to the world with their imagination. May this coloring book be a blank canvas for your brightest dreams and your most colorful adventures. May each stroke and every color bring a smile to your face and inspire new stories. May art accompany you on all journeys of life. Have fun coloring!

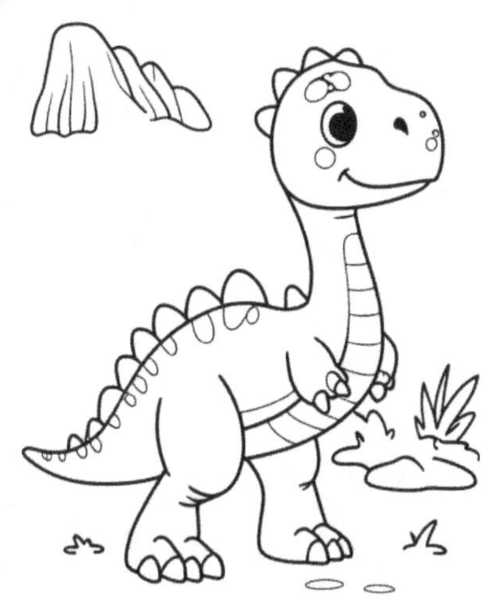 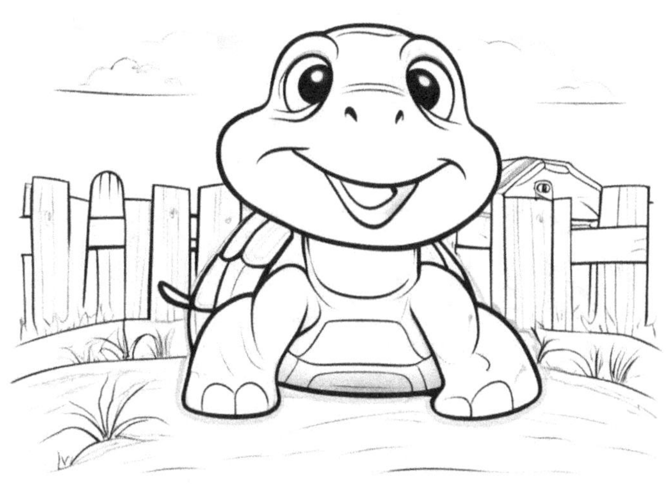

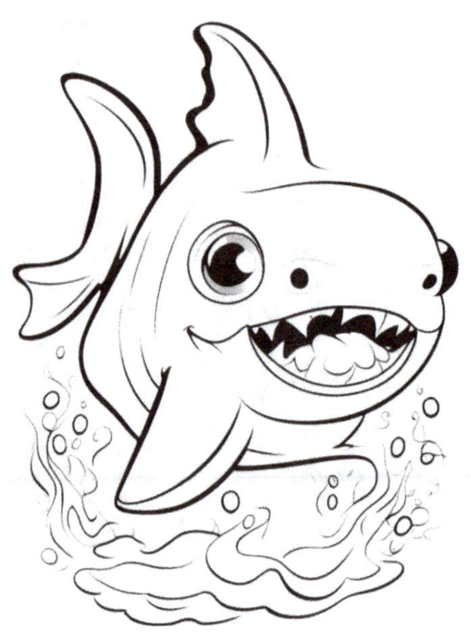

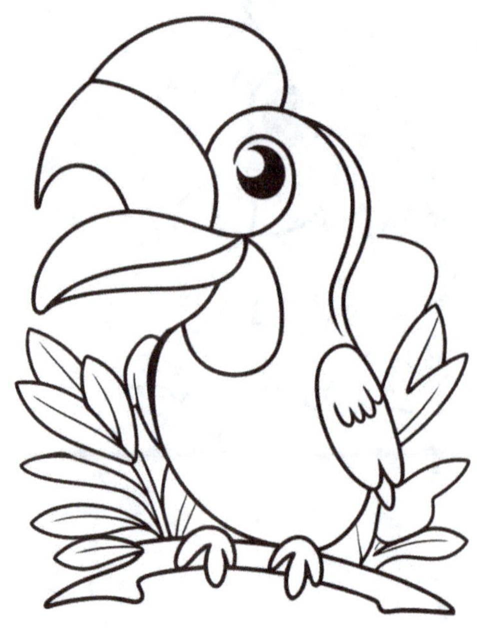

This Book Belongs To:

____

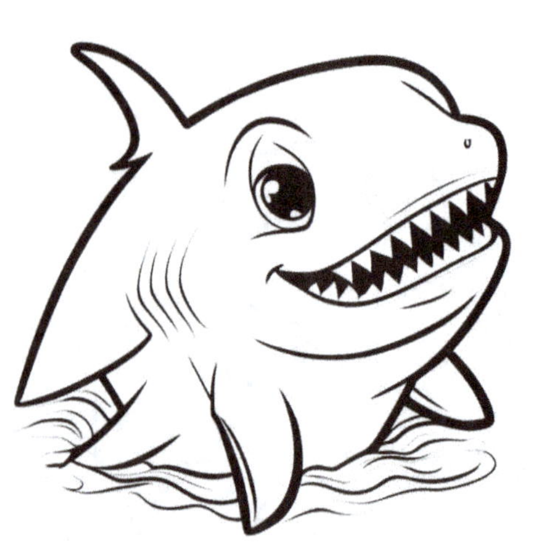

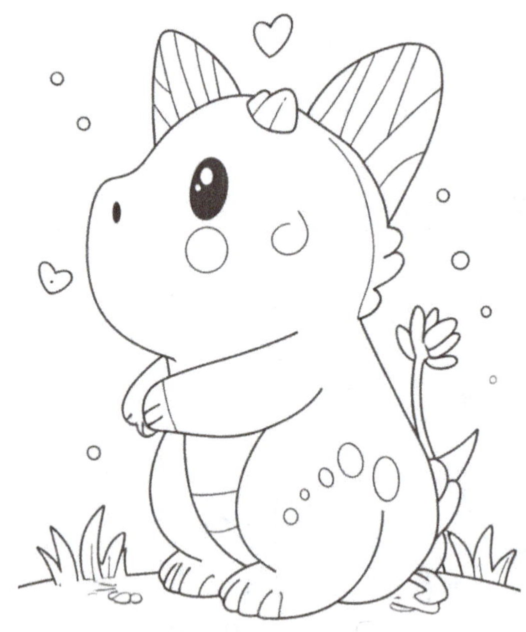

ALL RIGHTS RESERVED
2024

It is fundamental to understand your copyrights. This comprehensive guide provides essential information for authors on how to protect their intellectual property and ensure that their work is recognized and respected.

M.B.P.©

Márcio Bittencourt publications

Test Color Page.

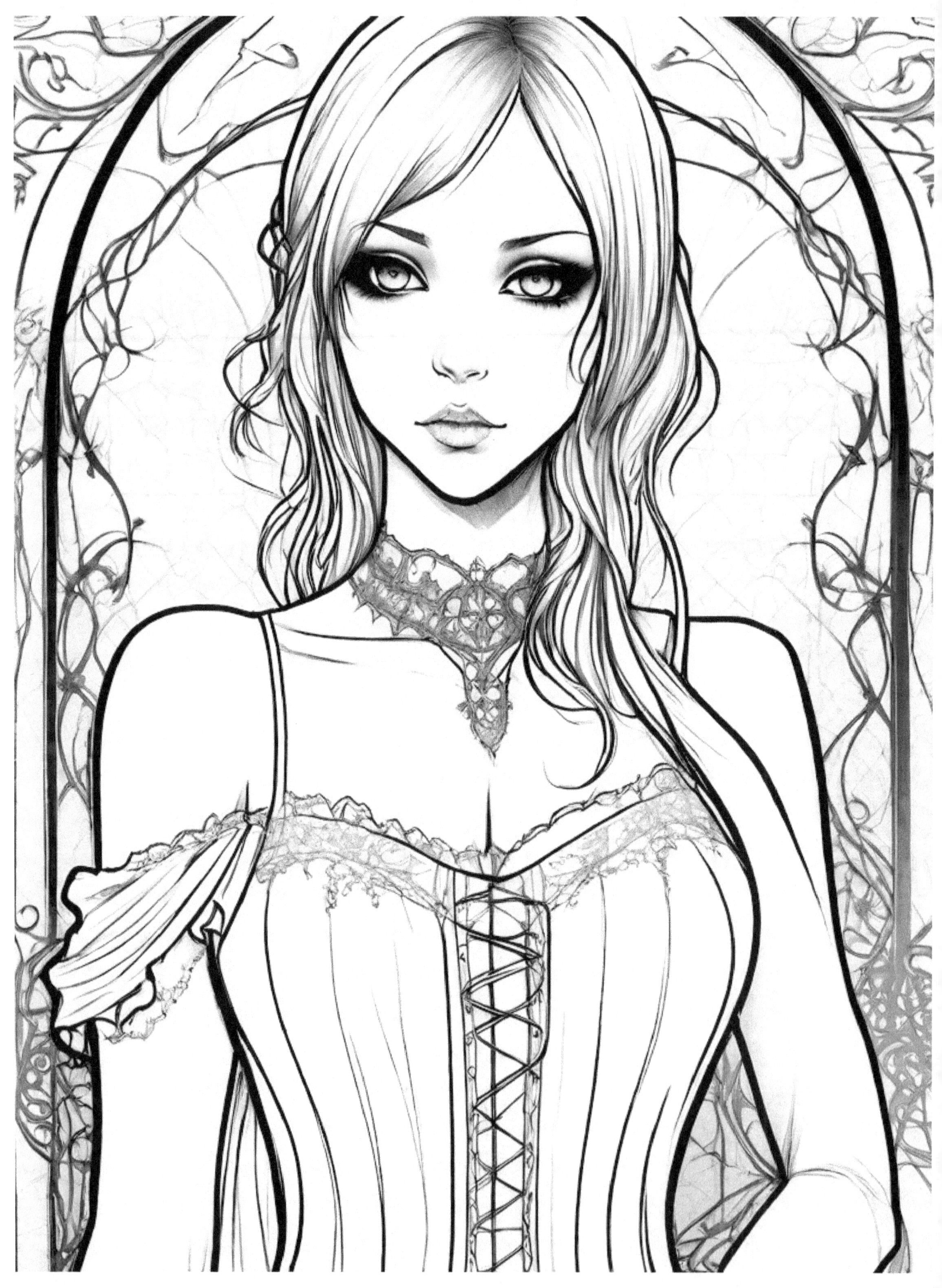

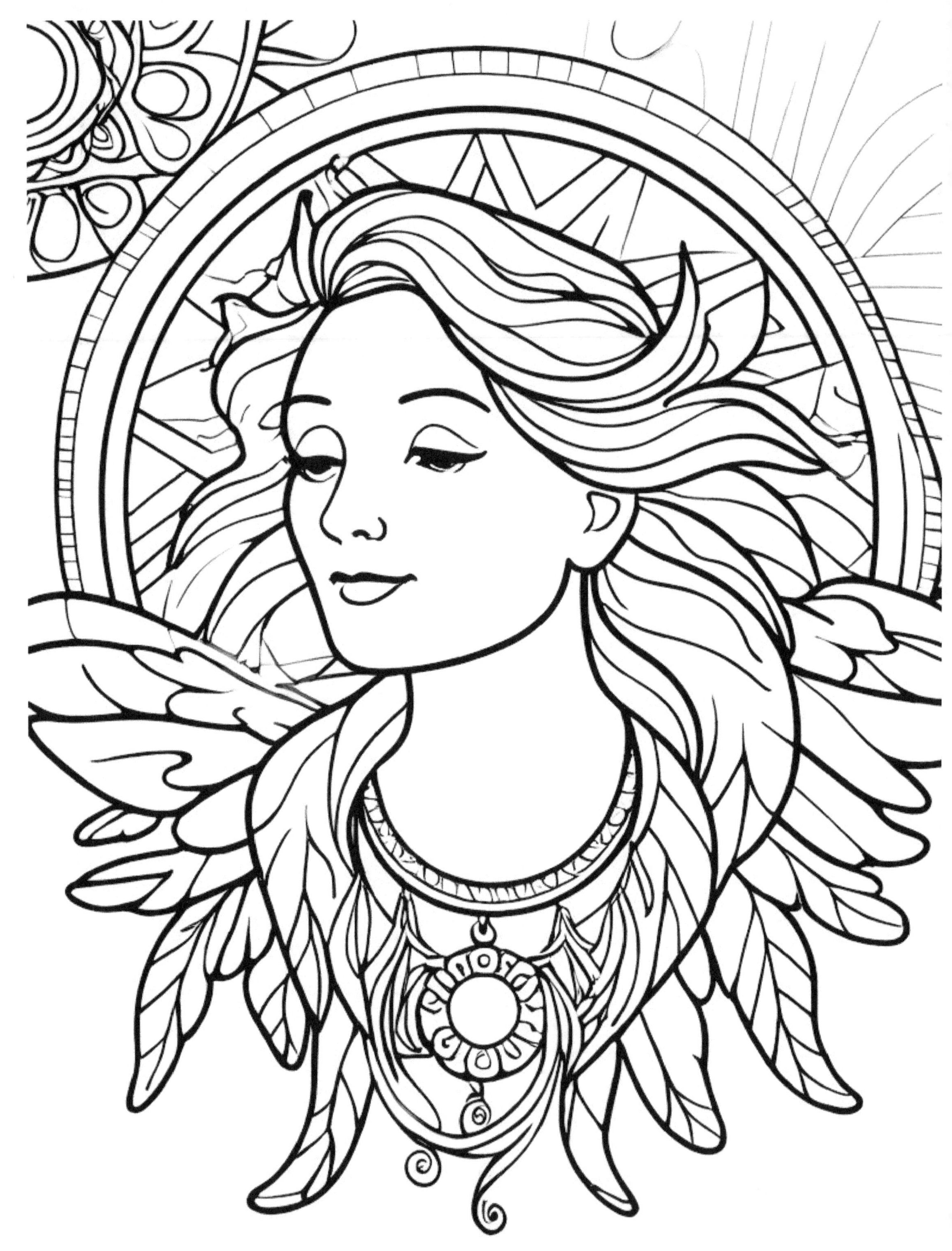

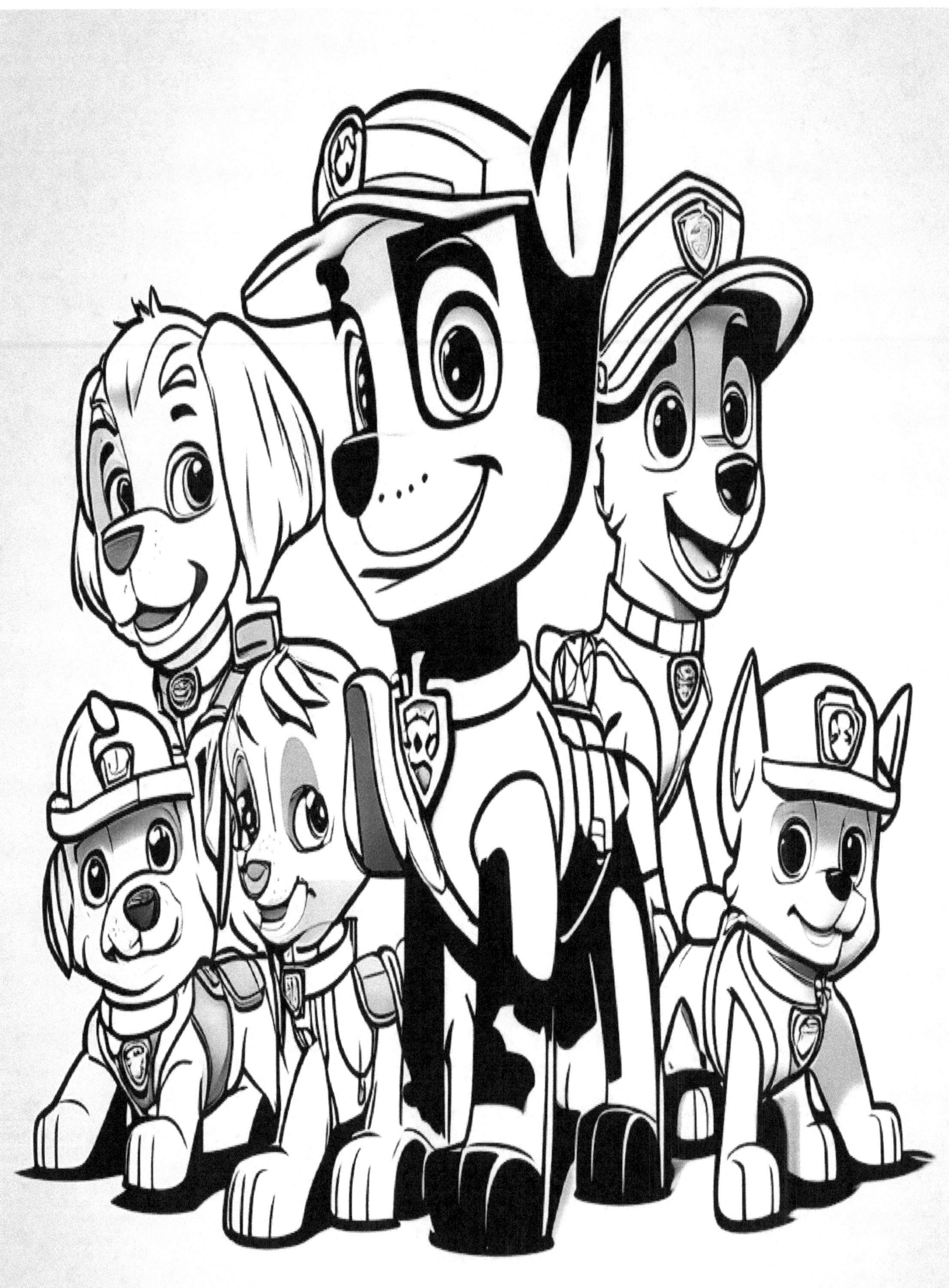

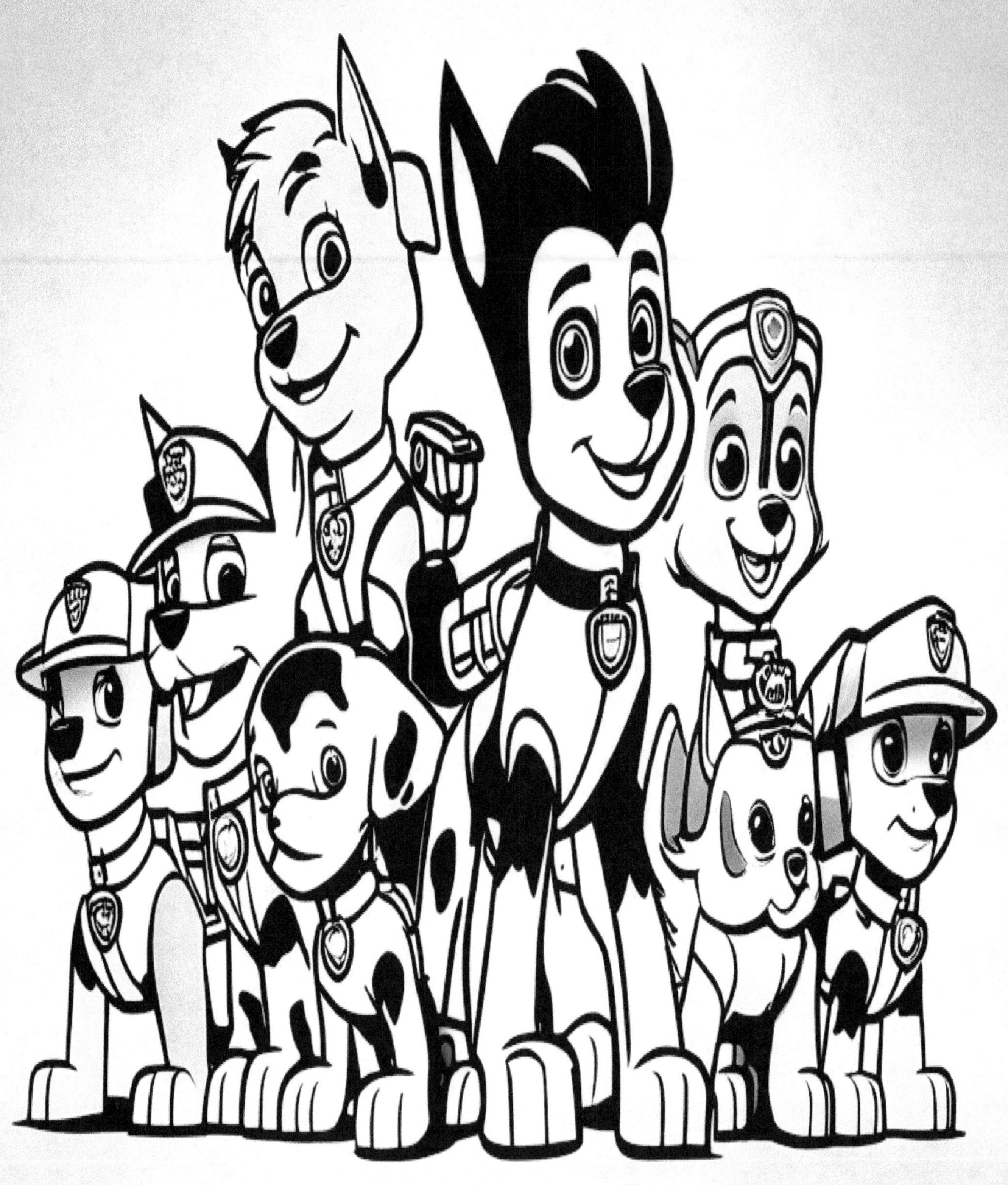

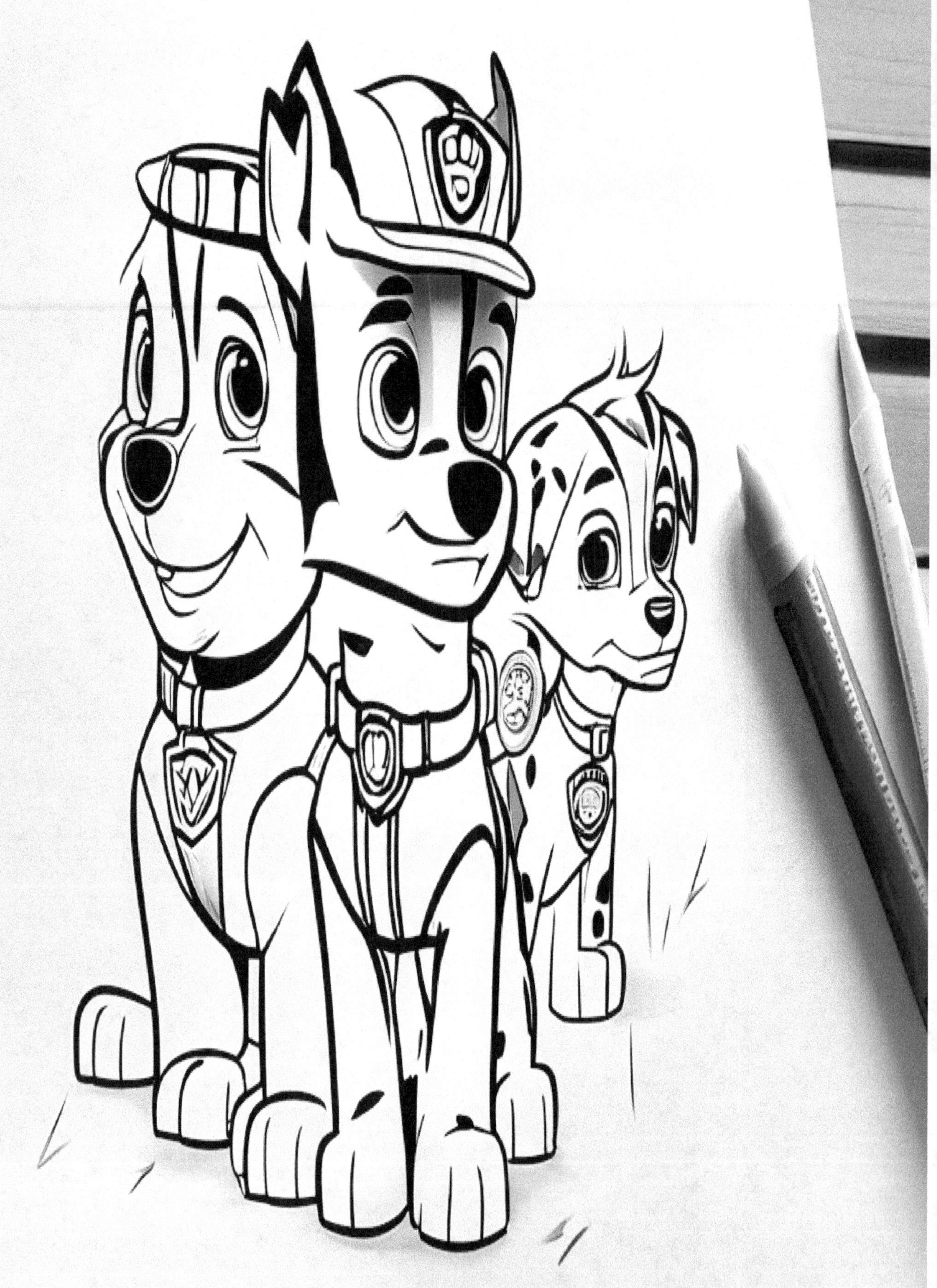

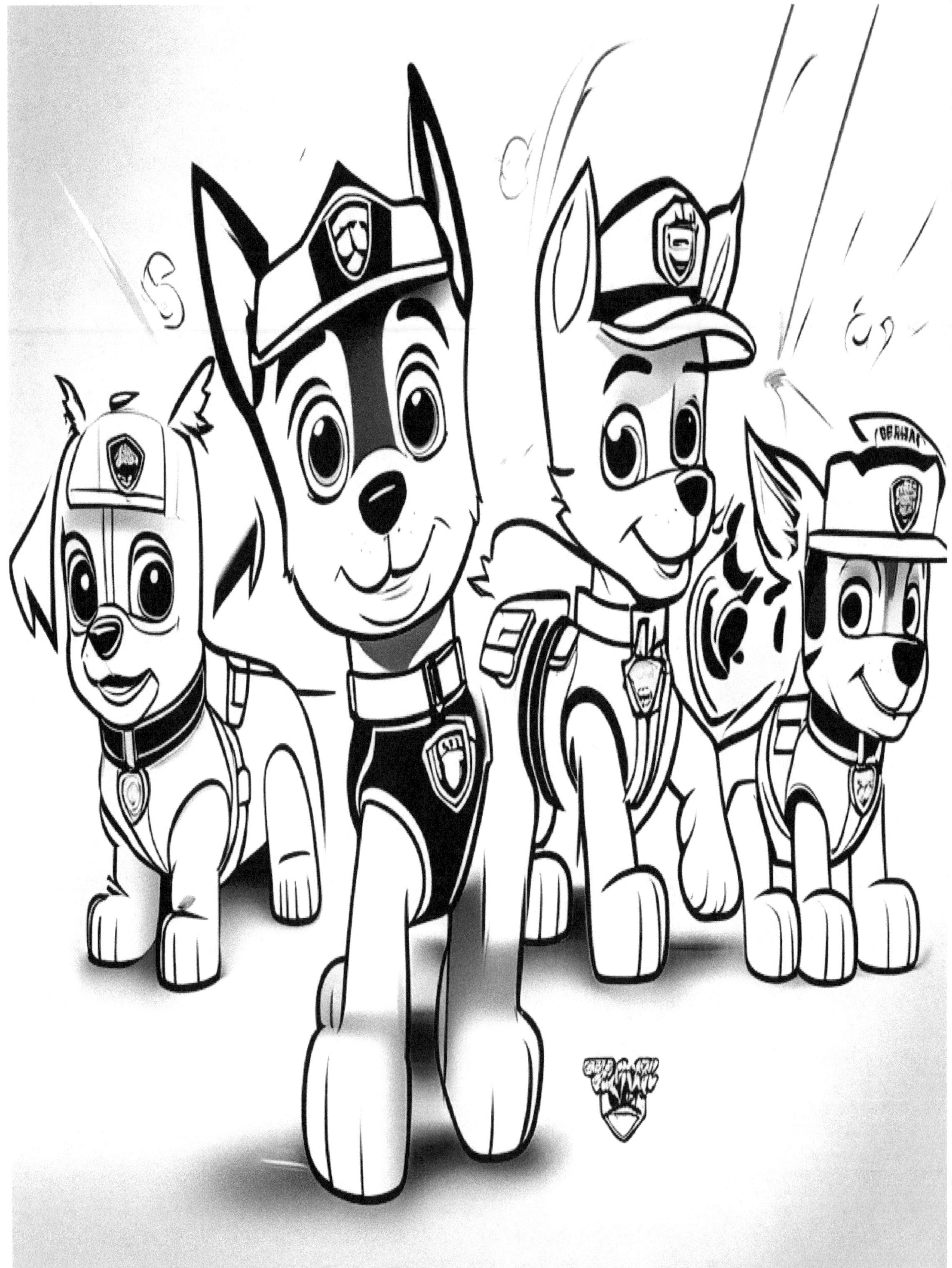

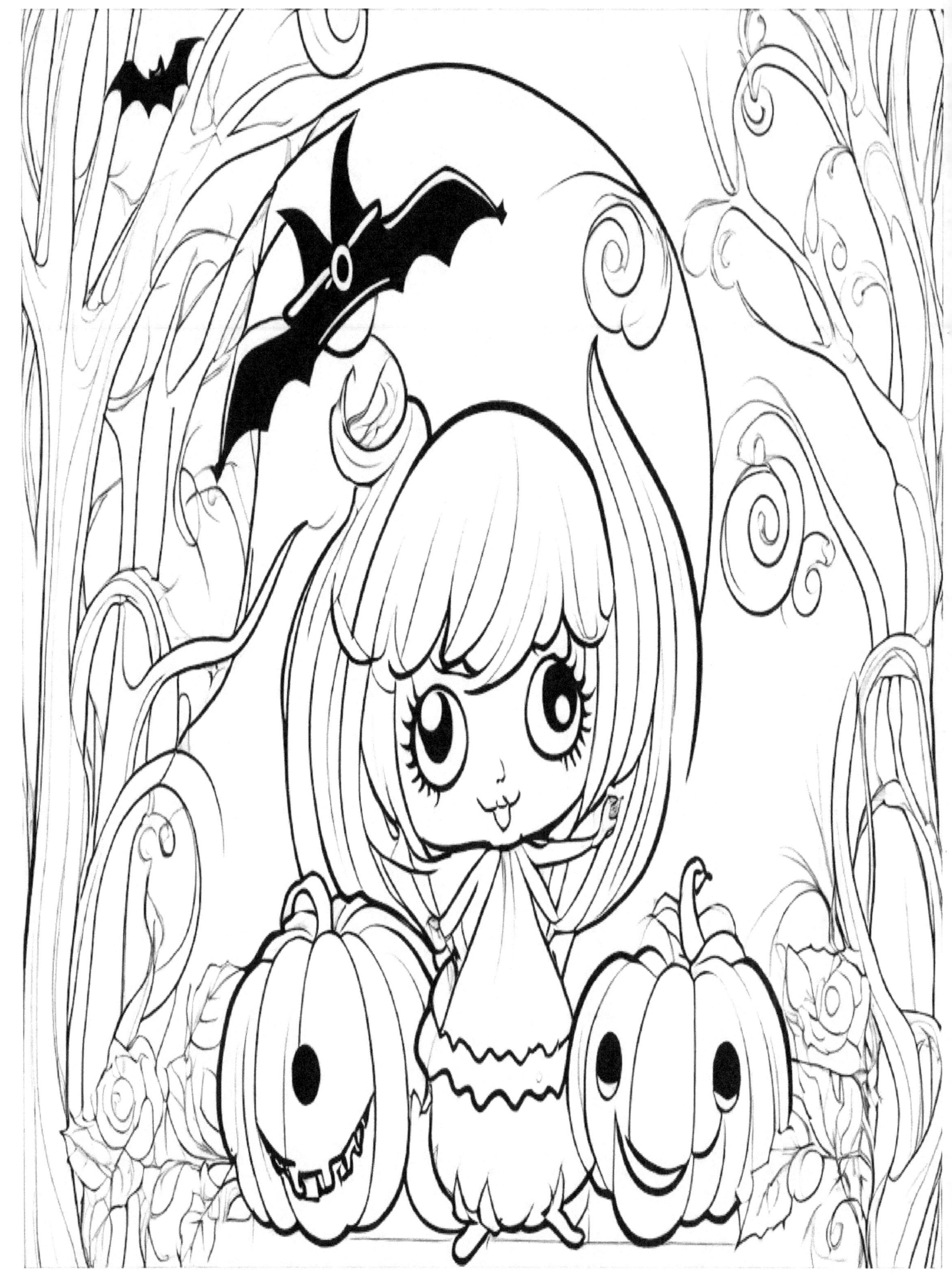

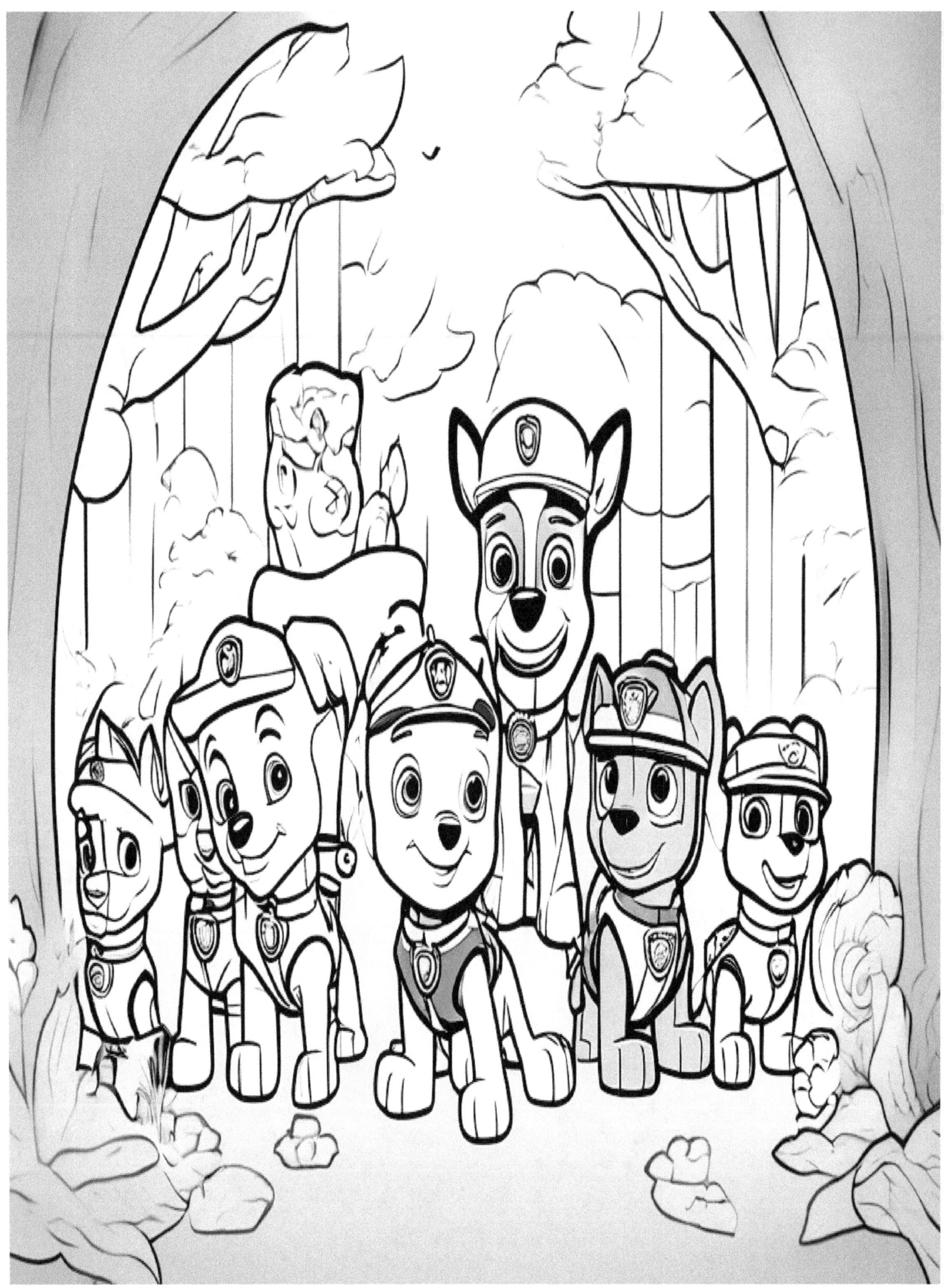

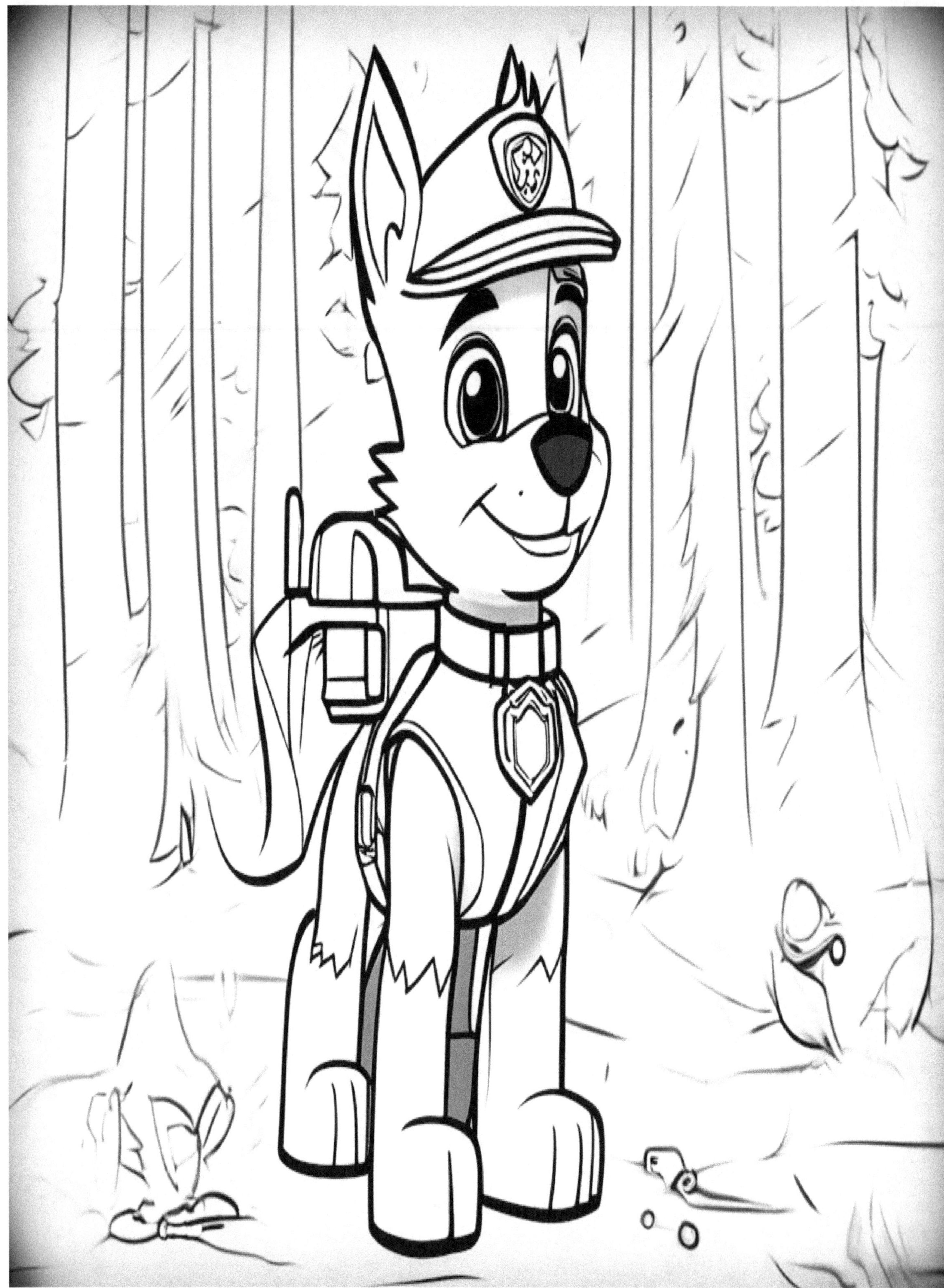

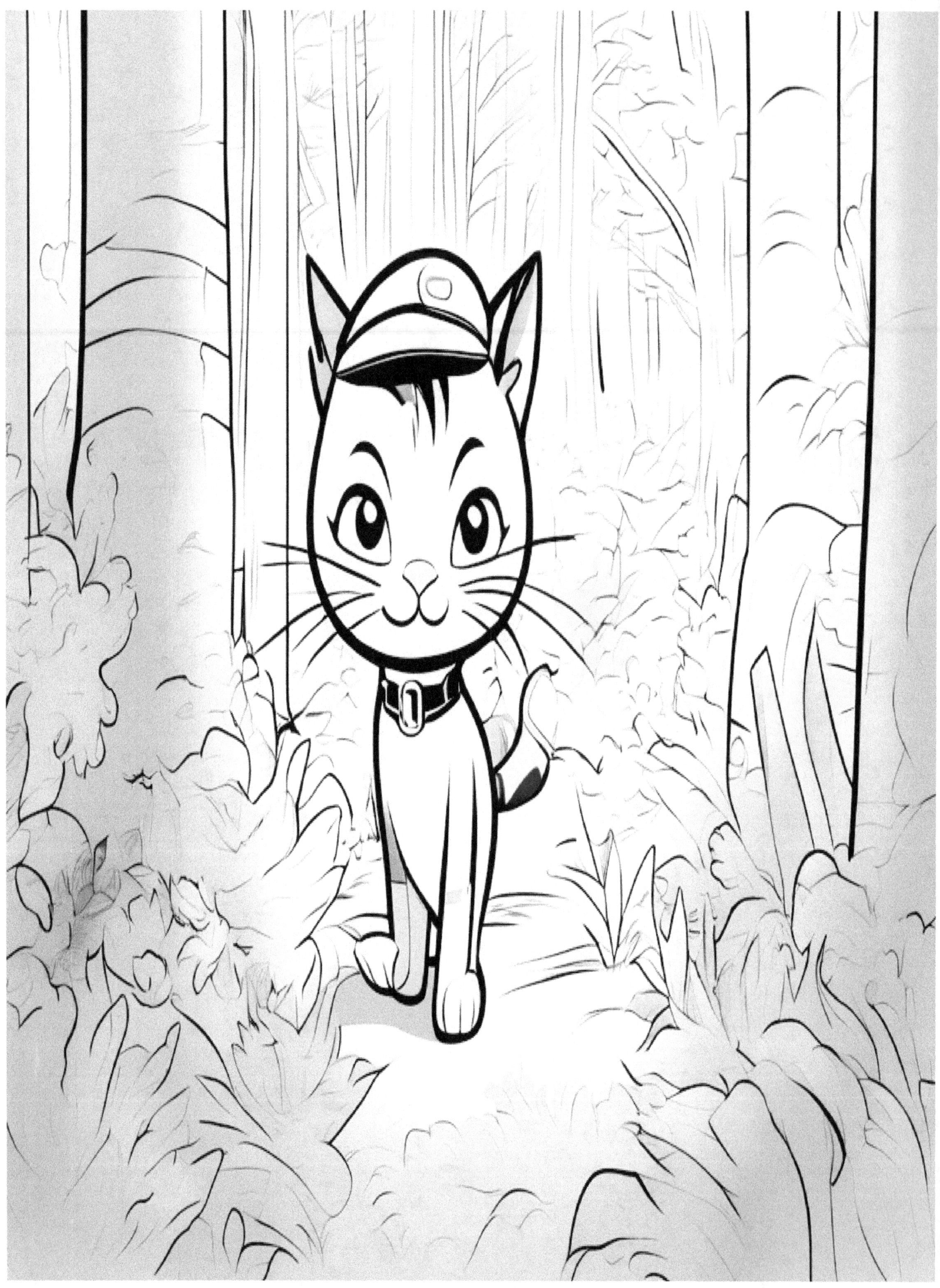

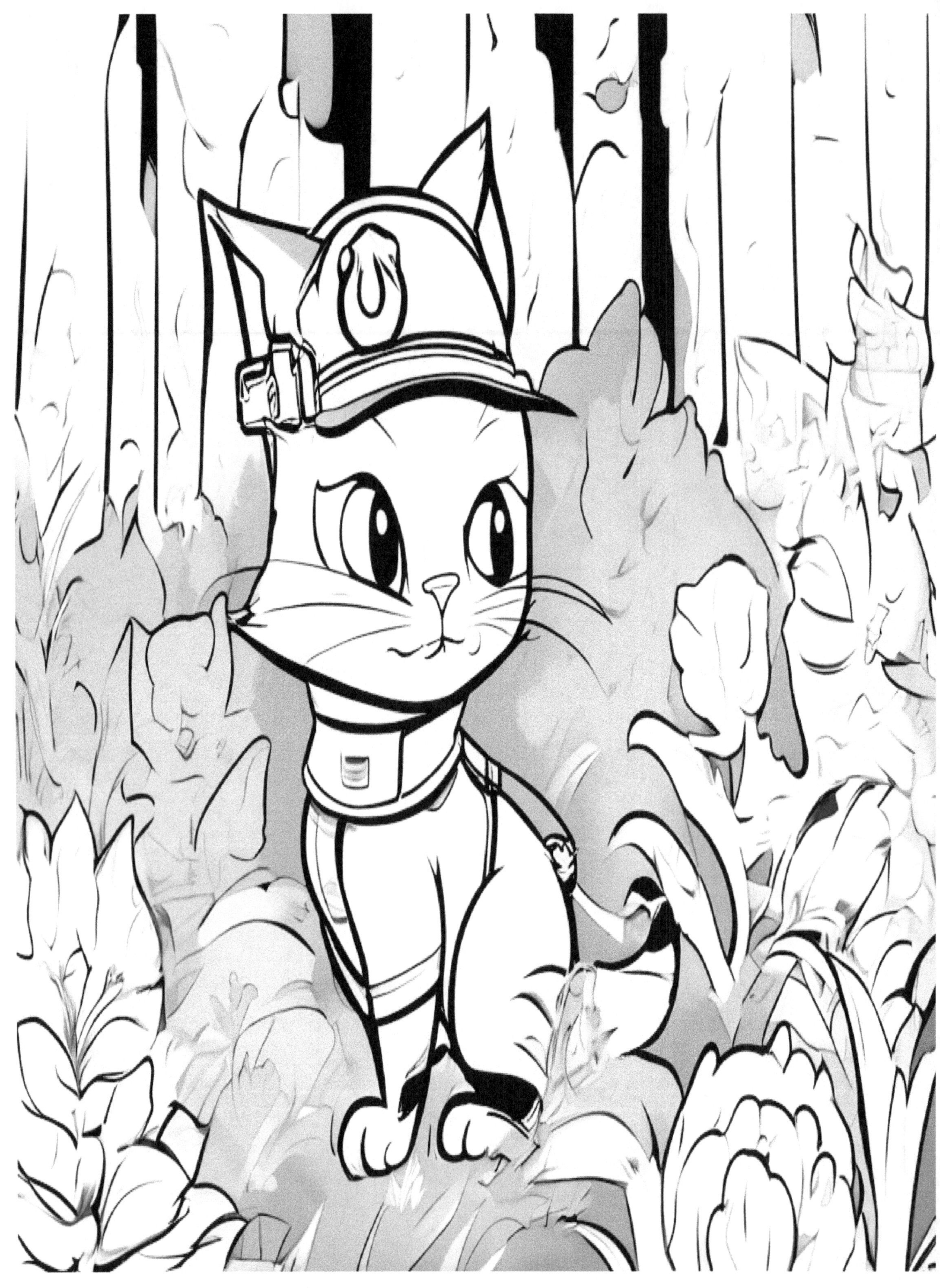

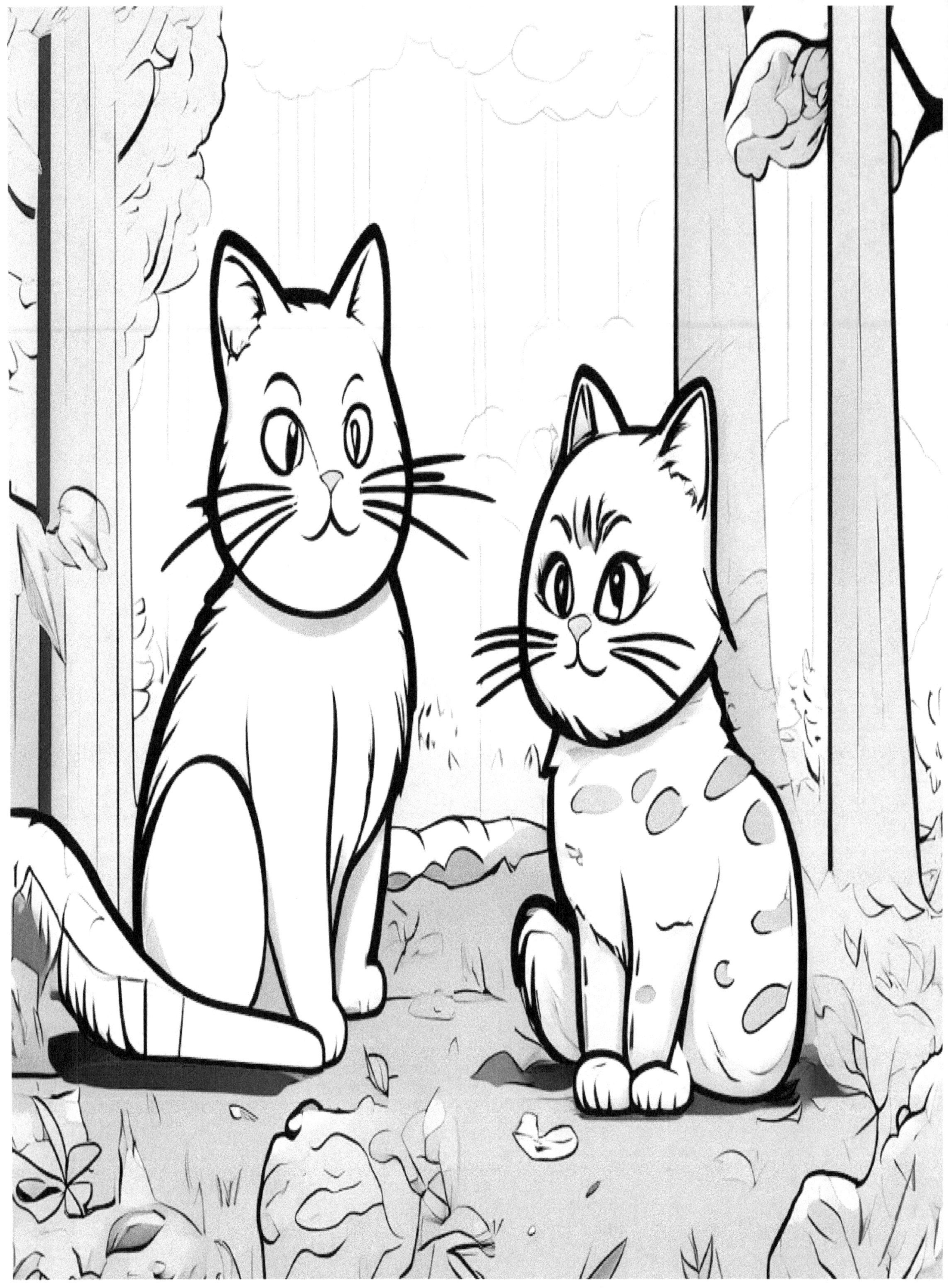

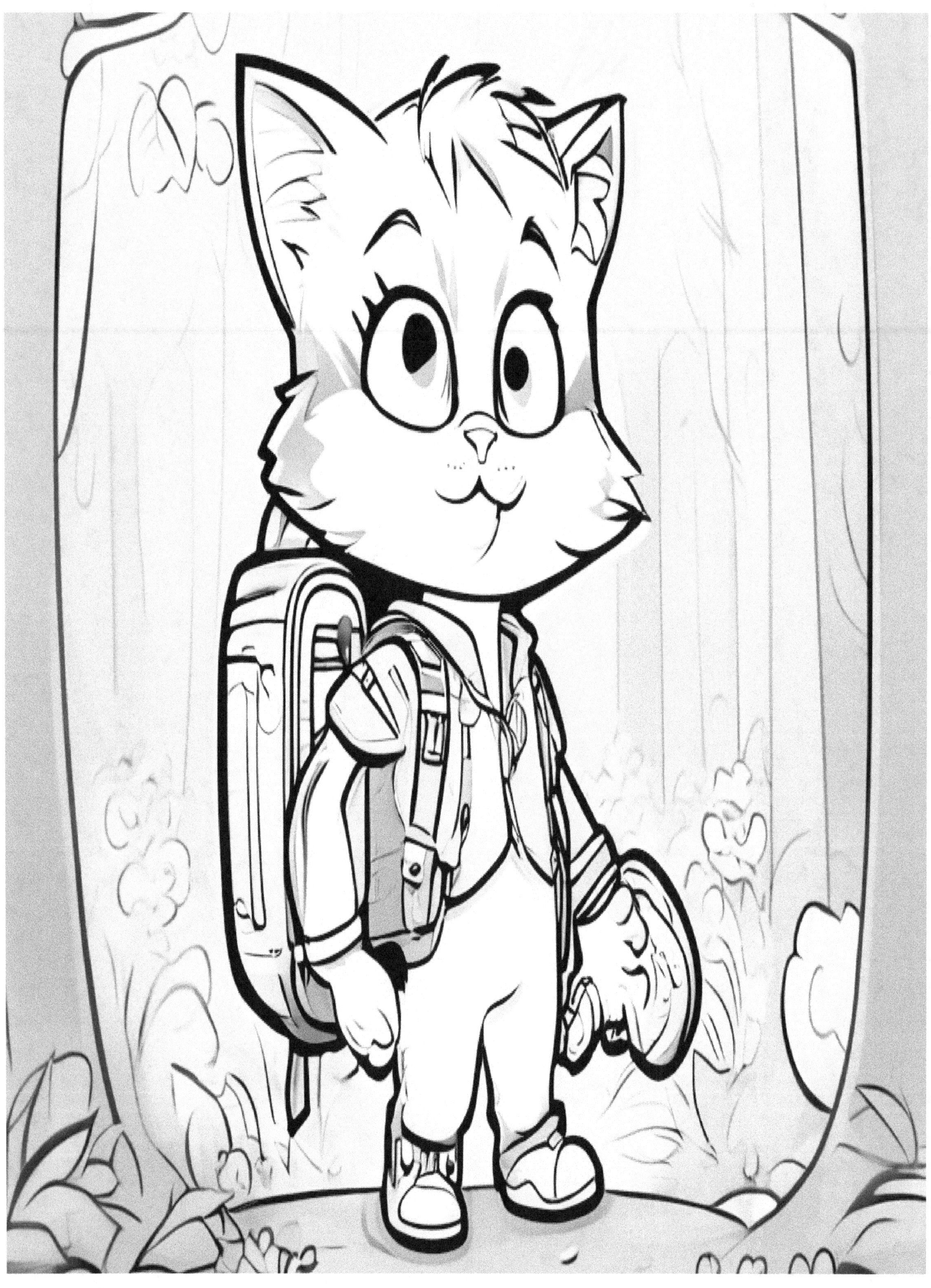

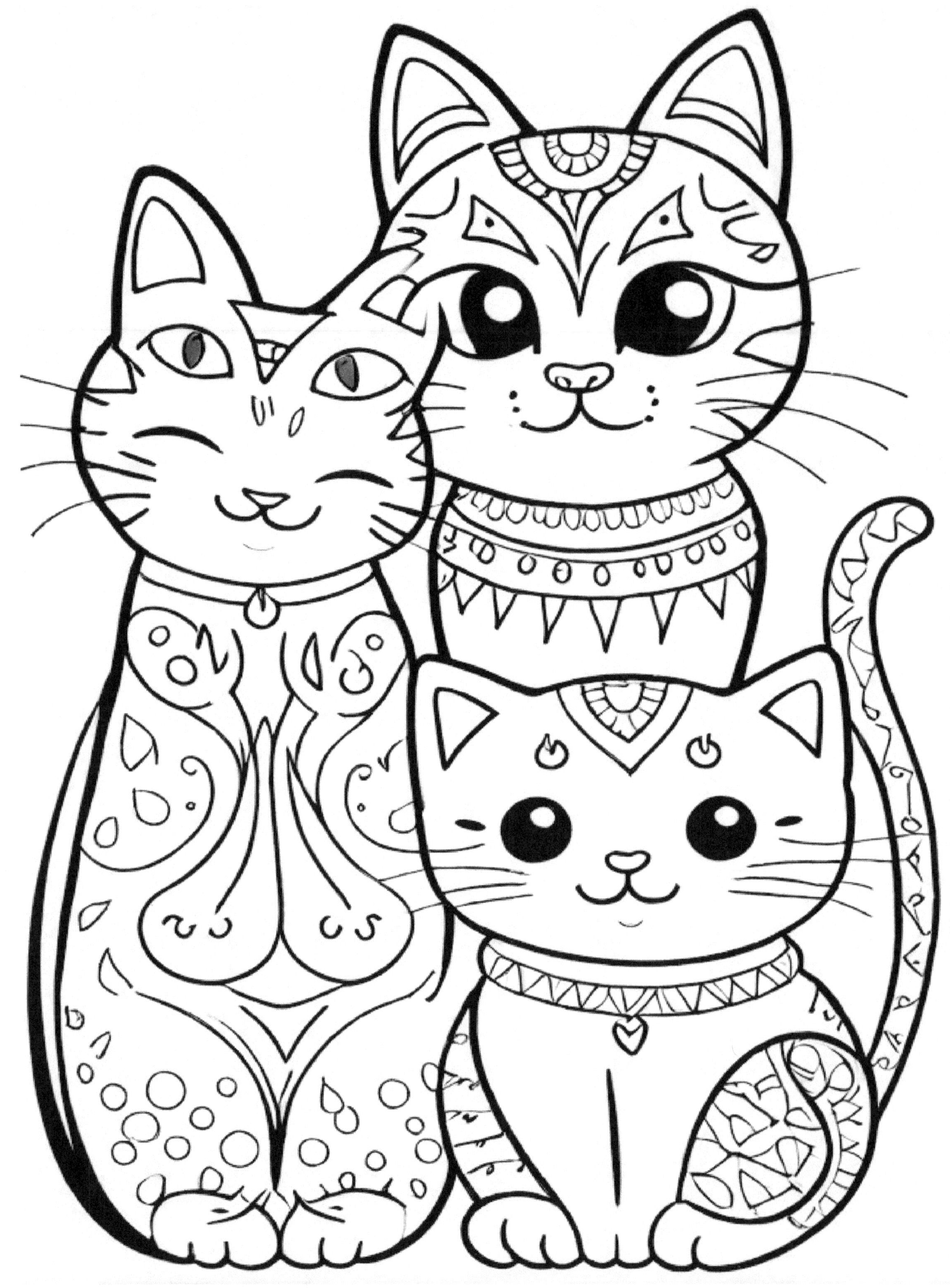

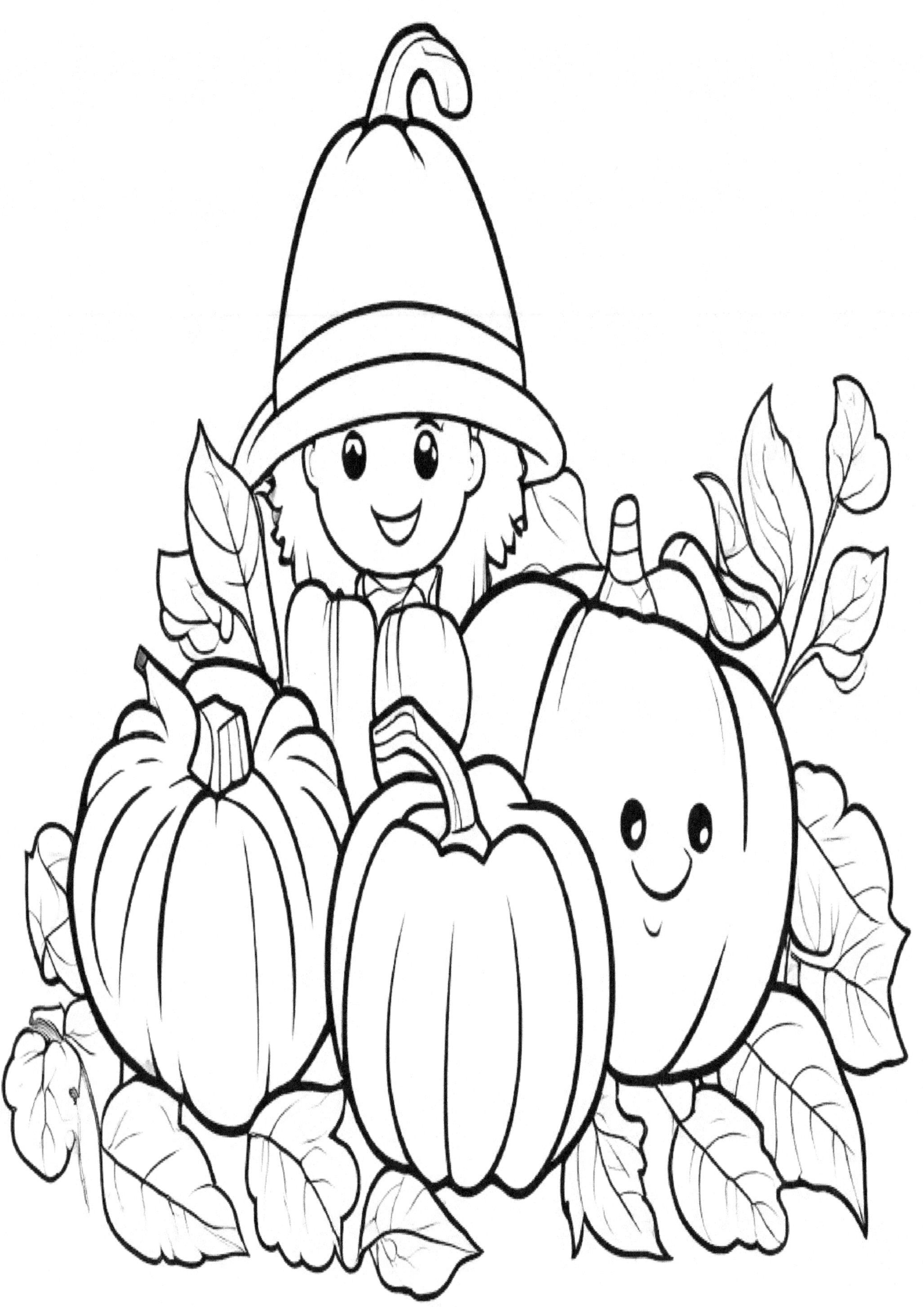

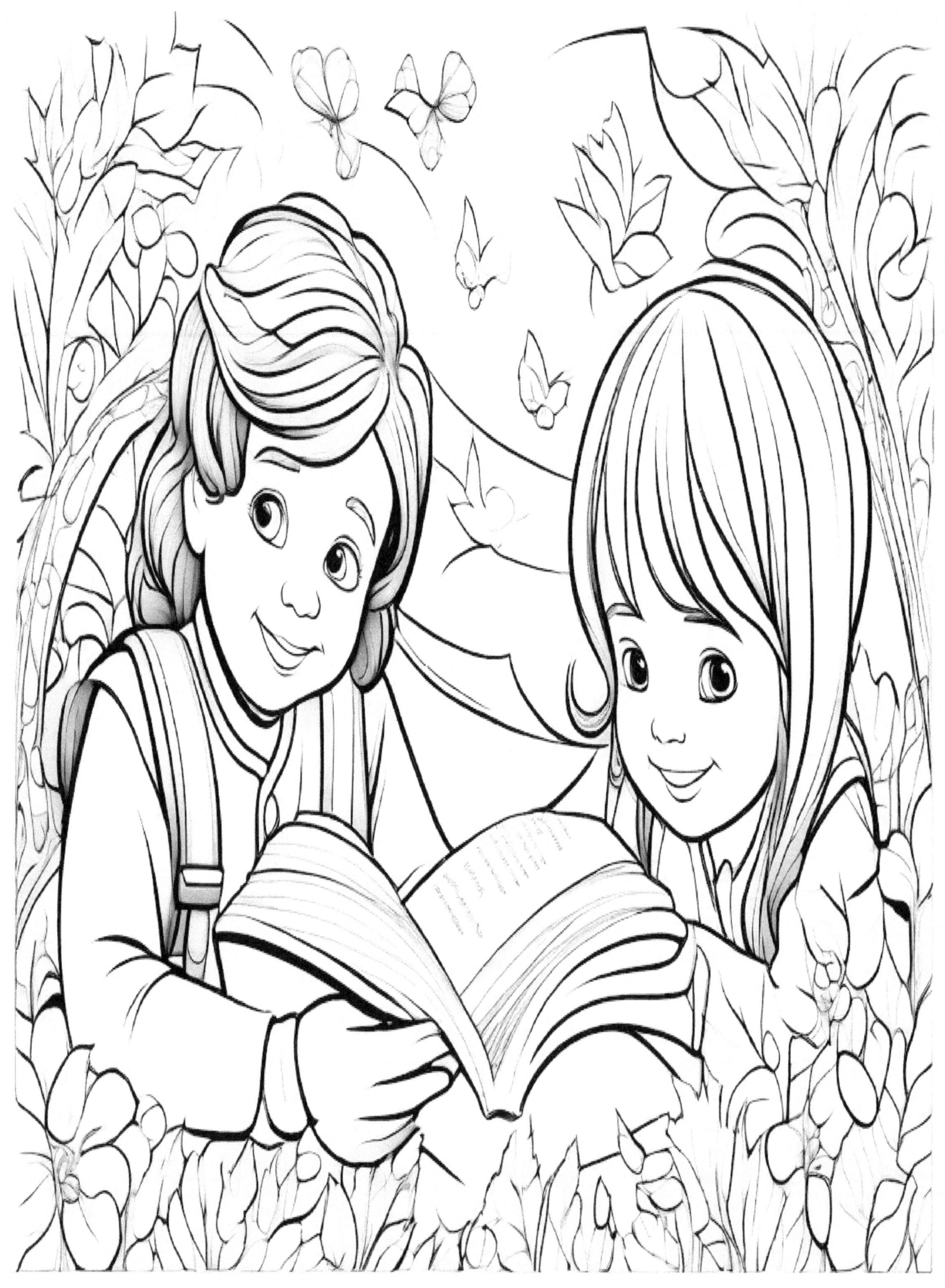

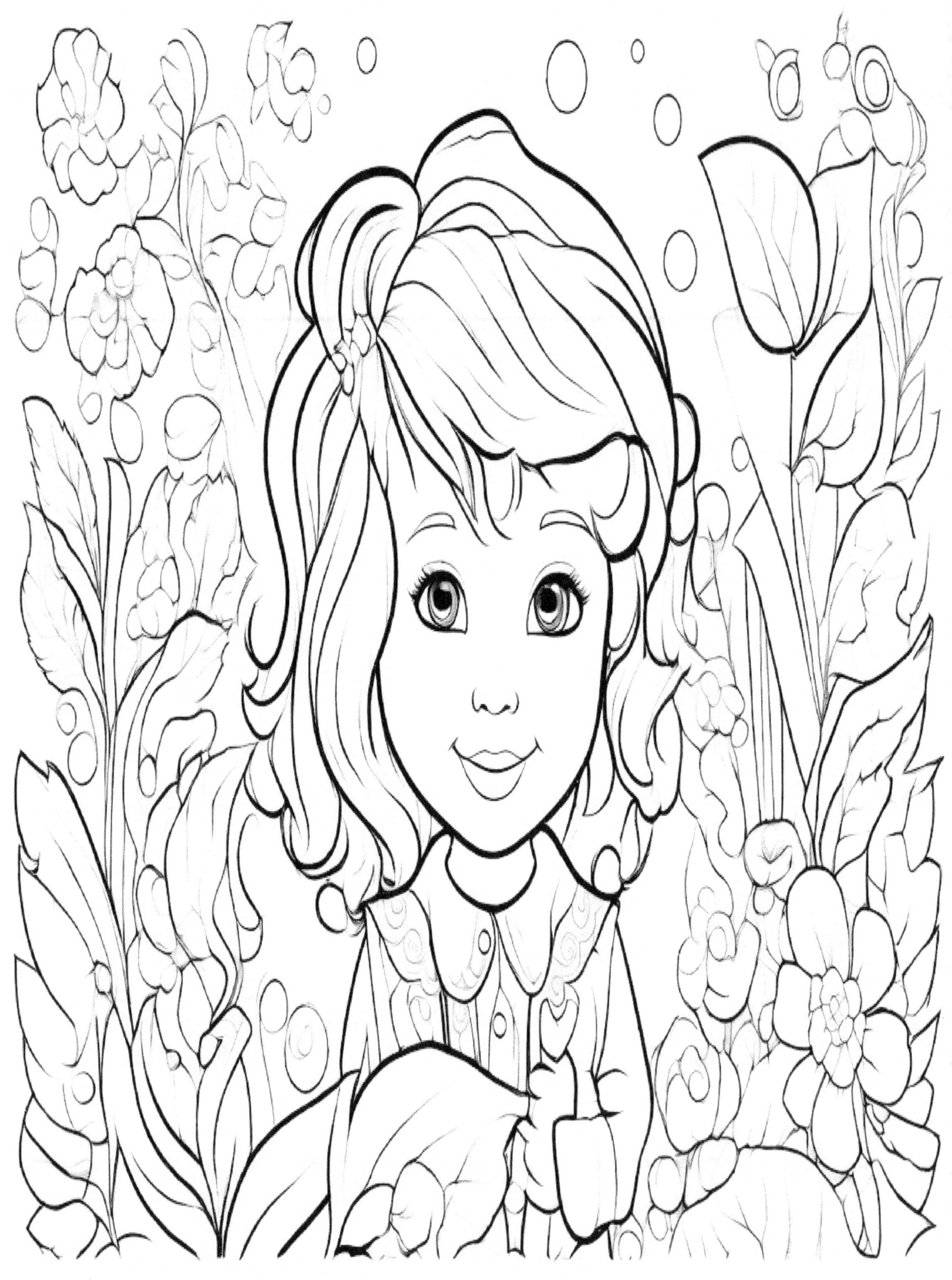

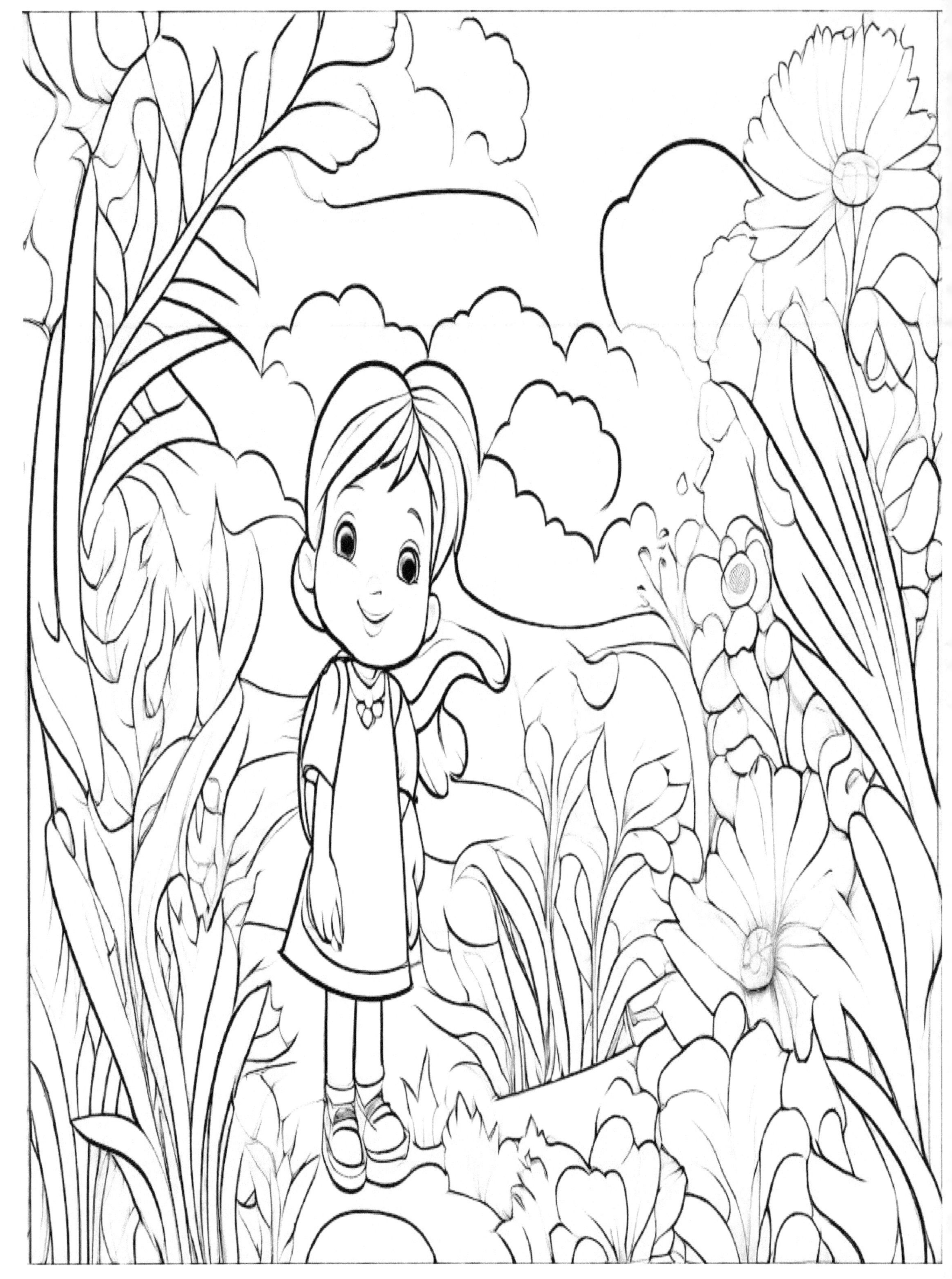

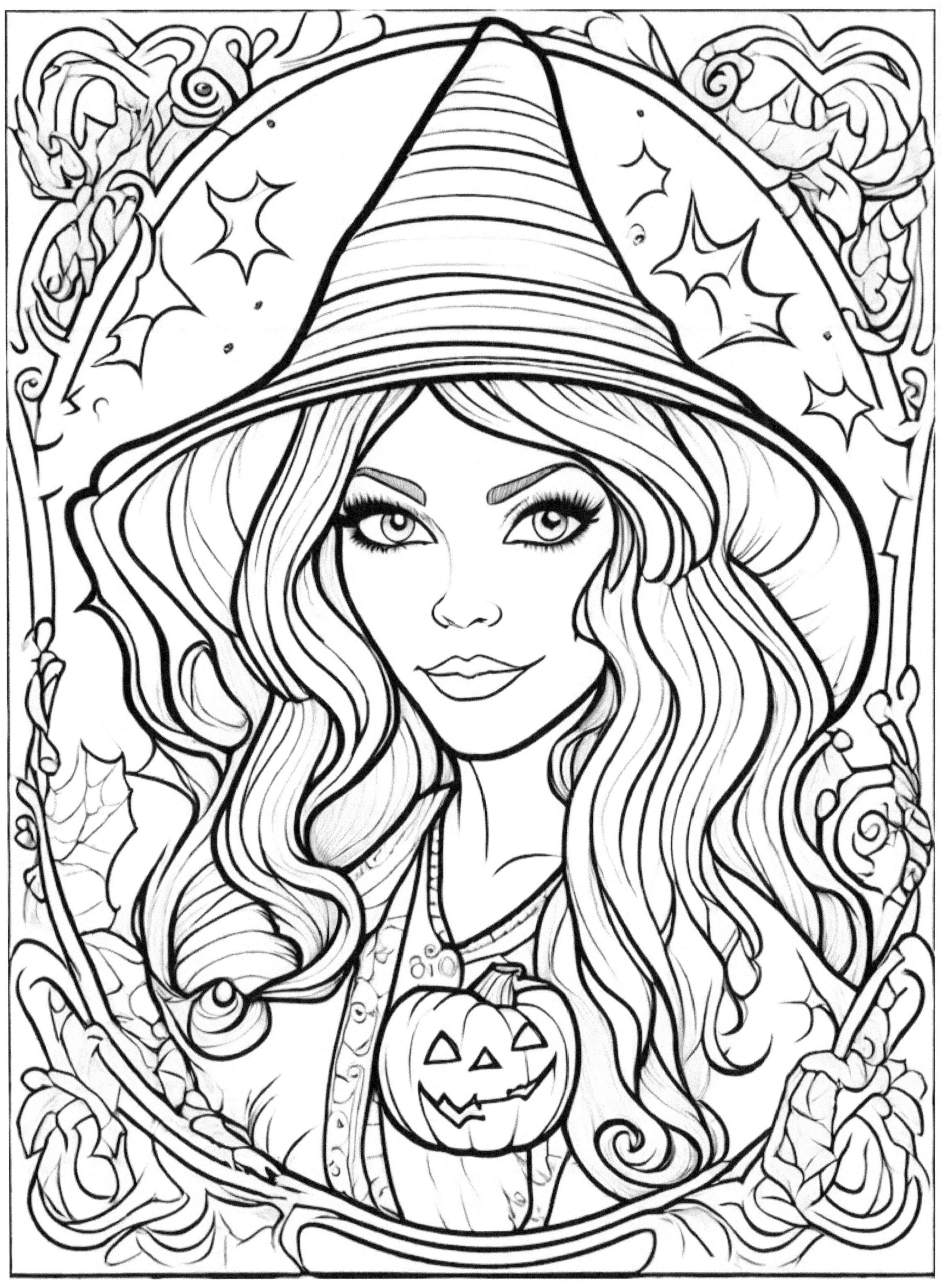

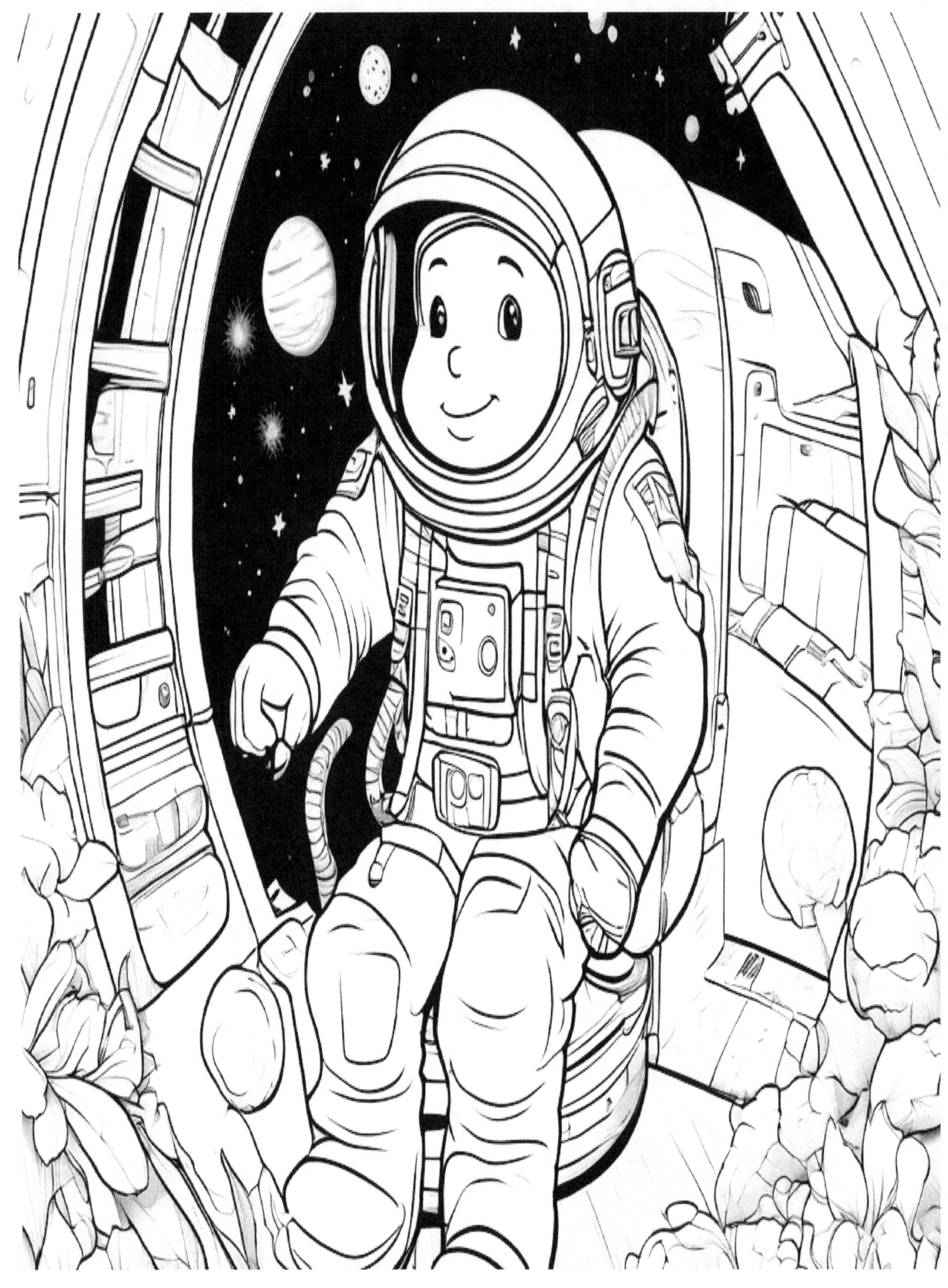

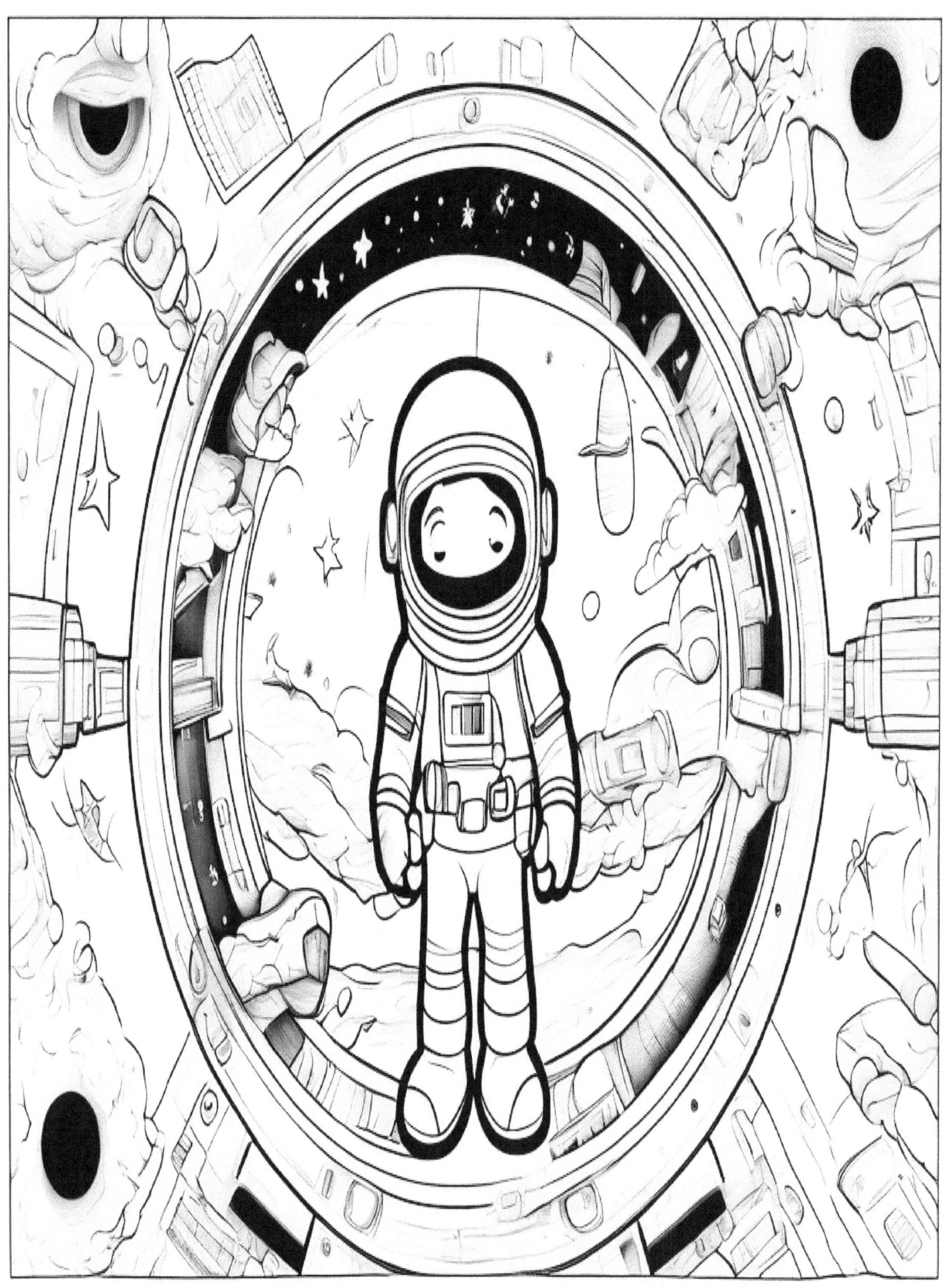

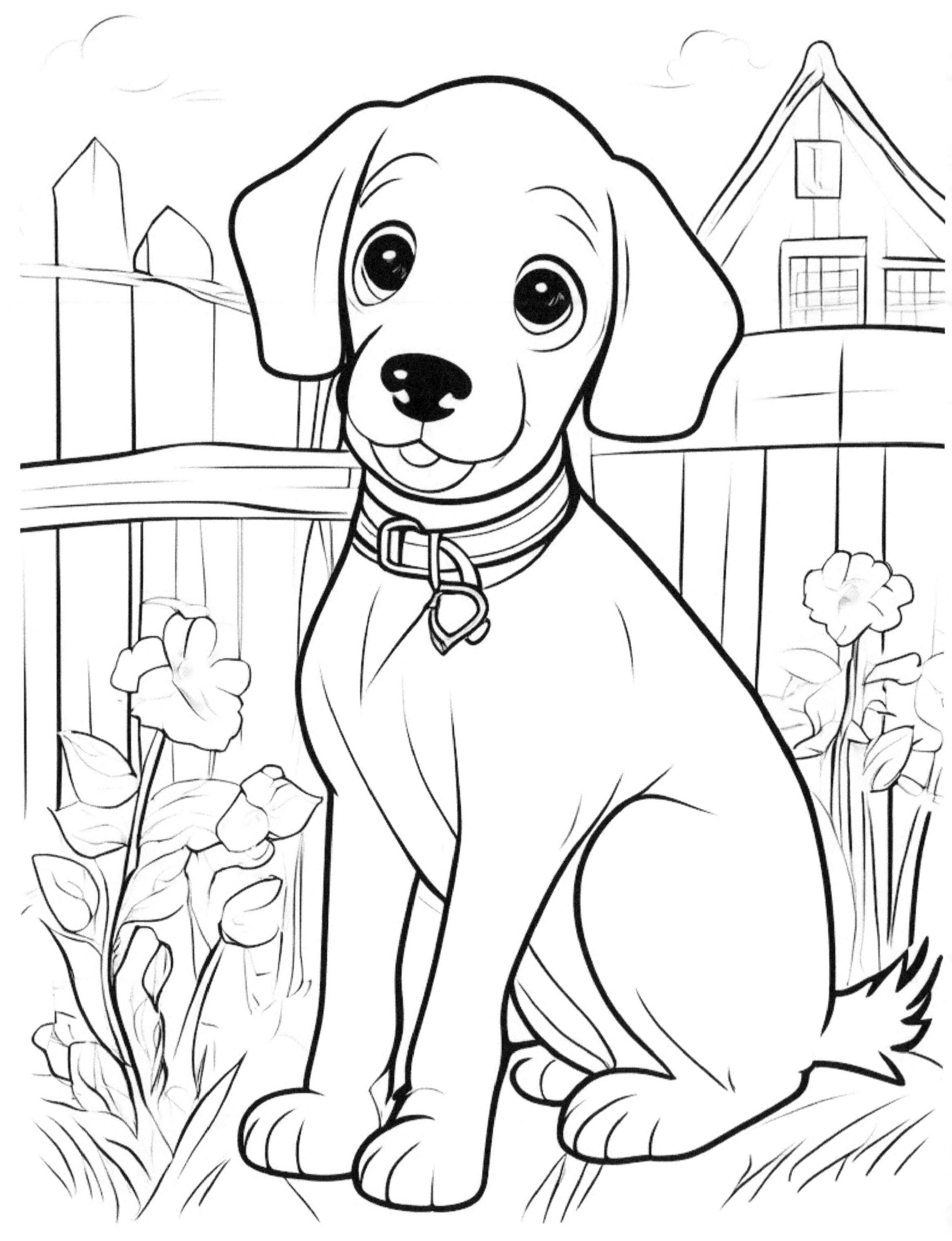

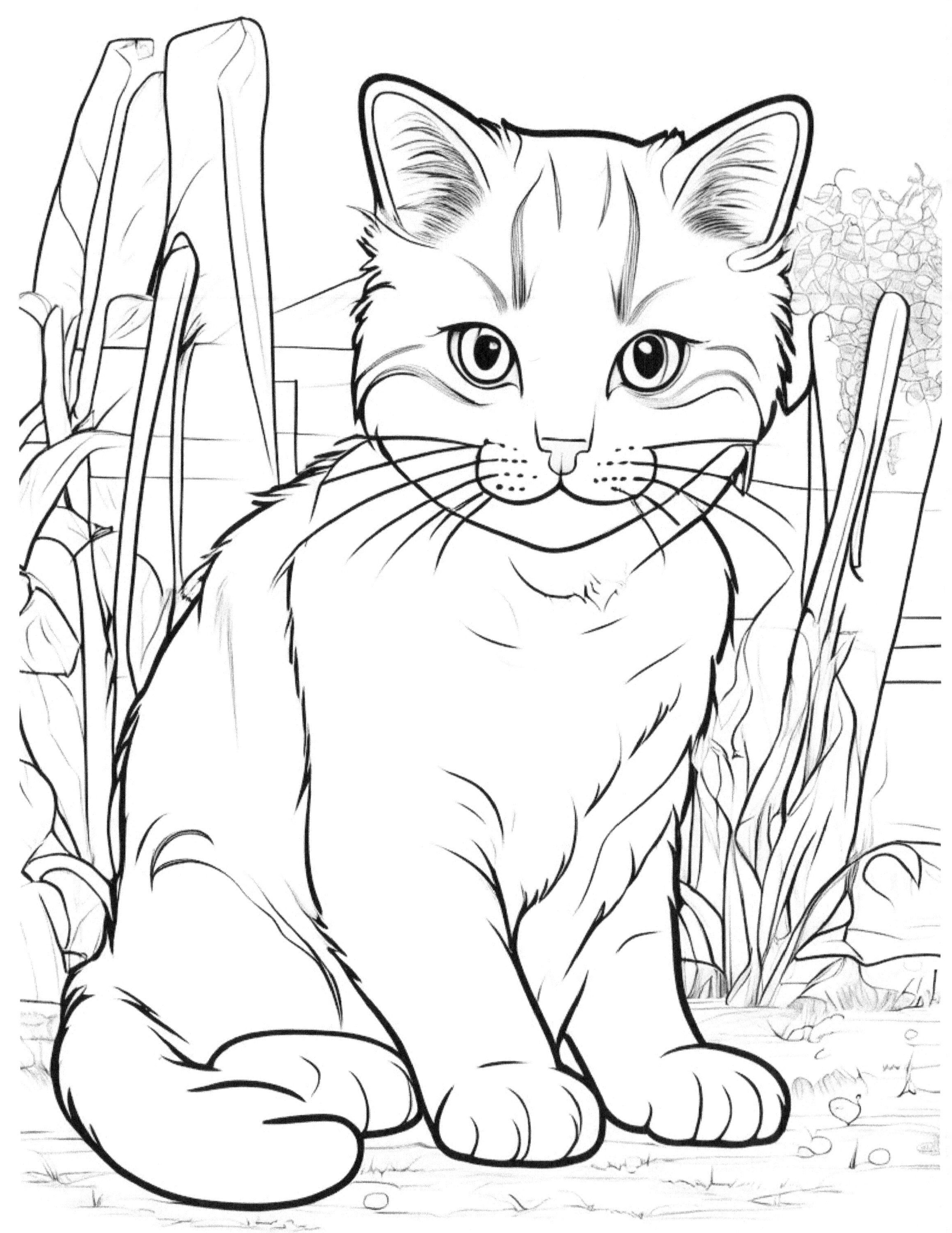

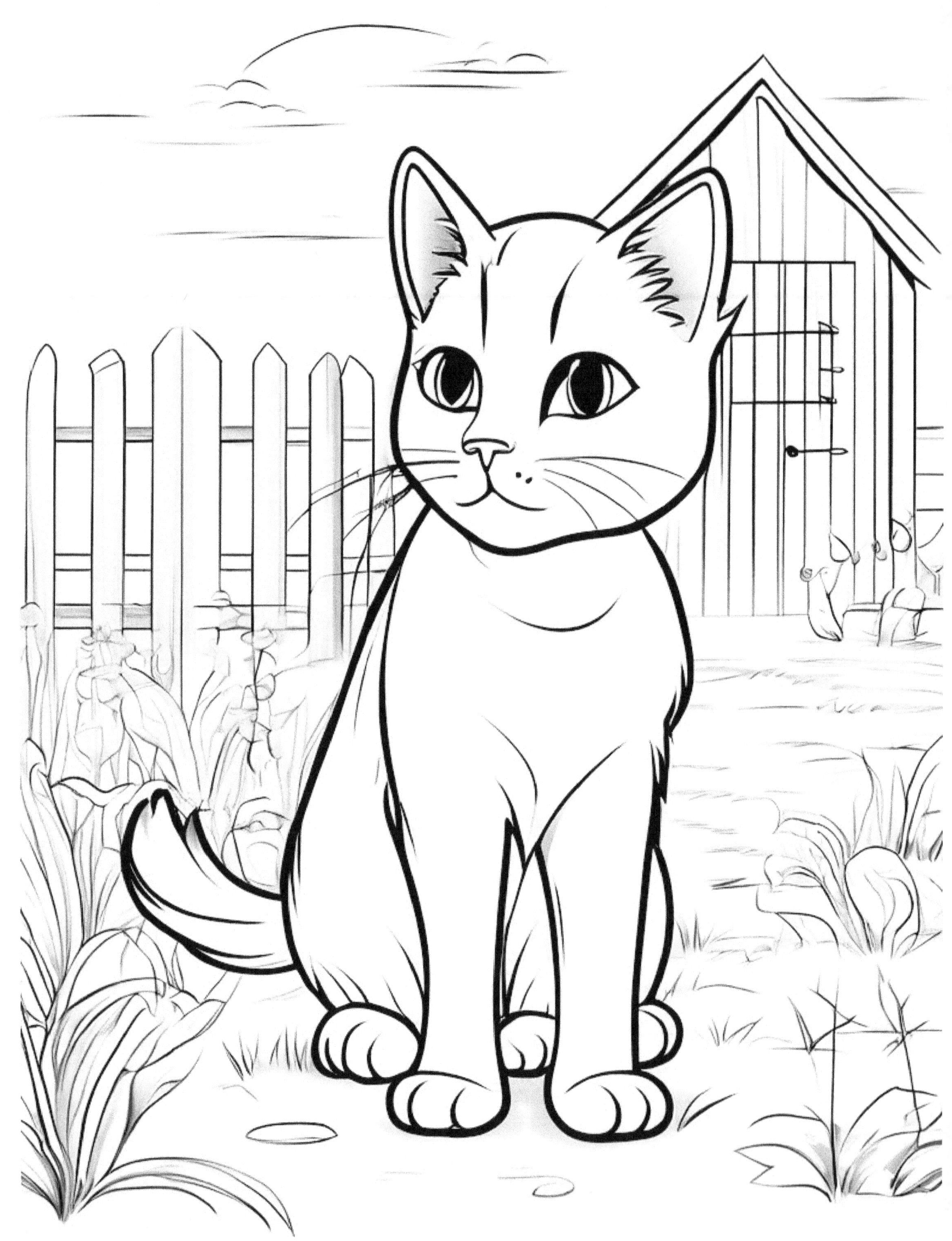

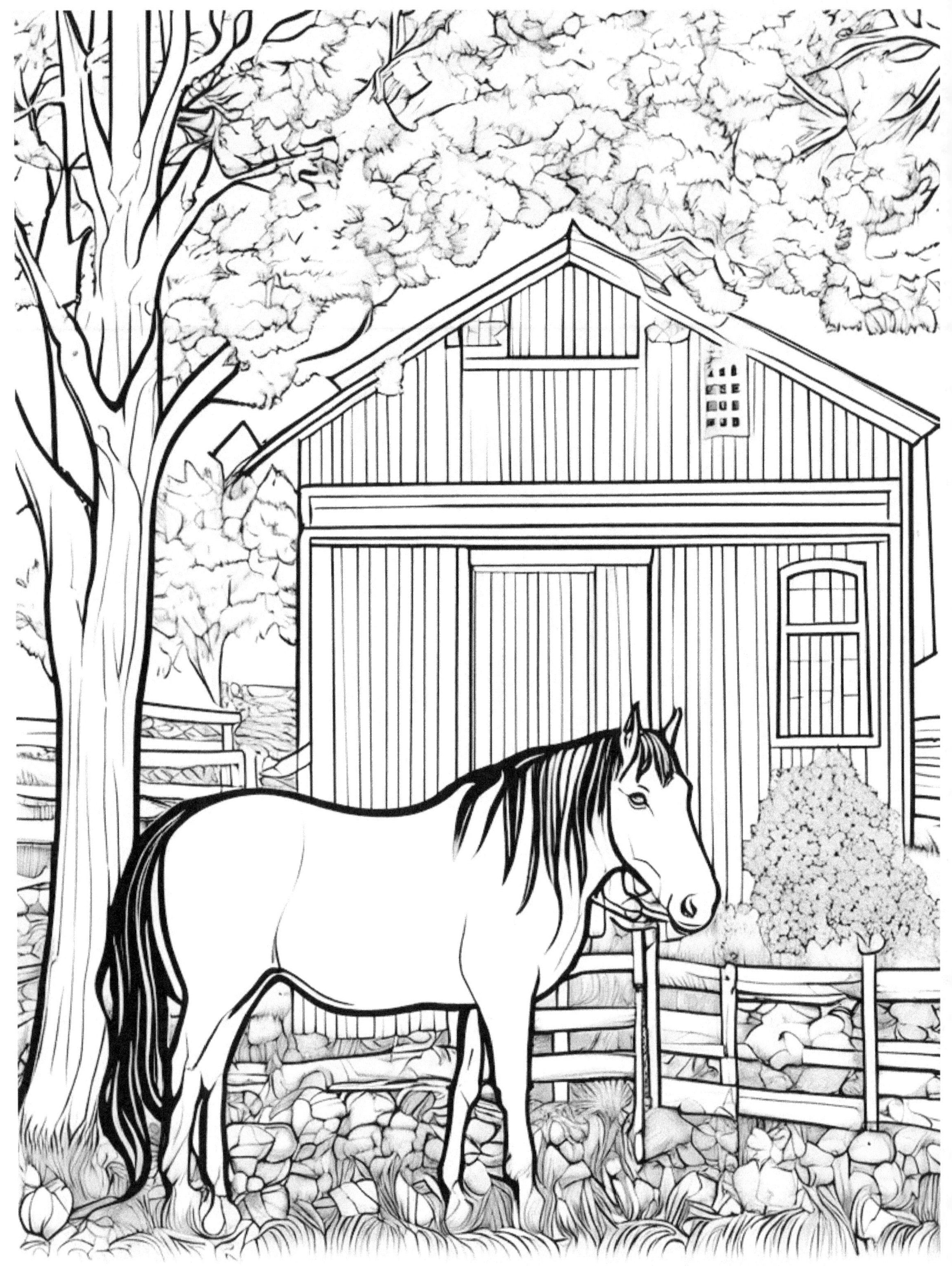

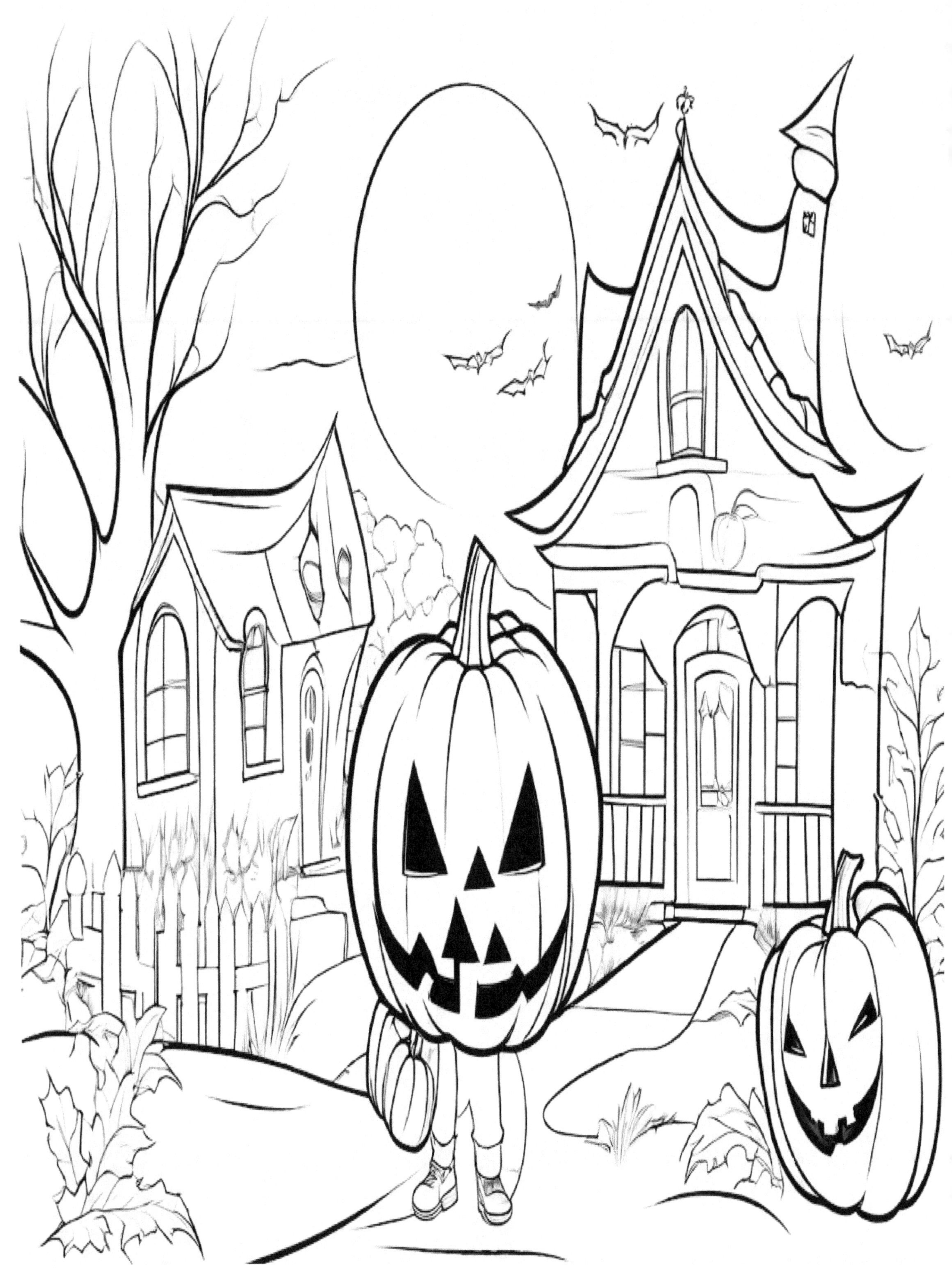

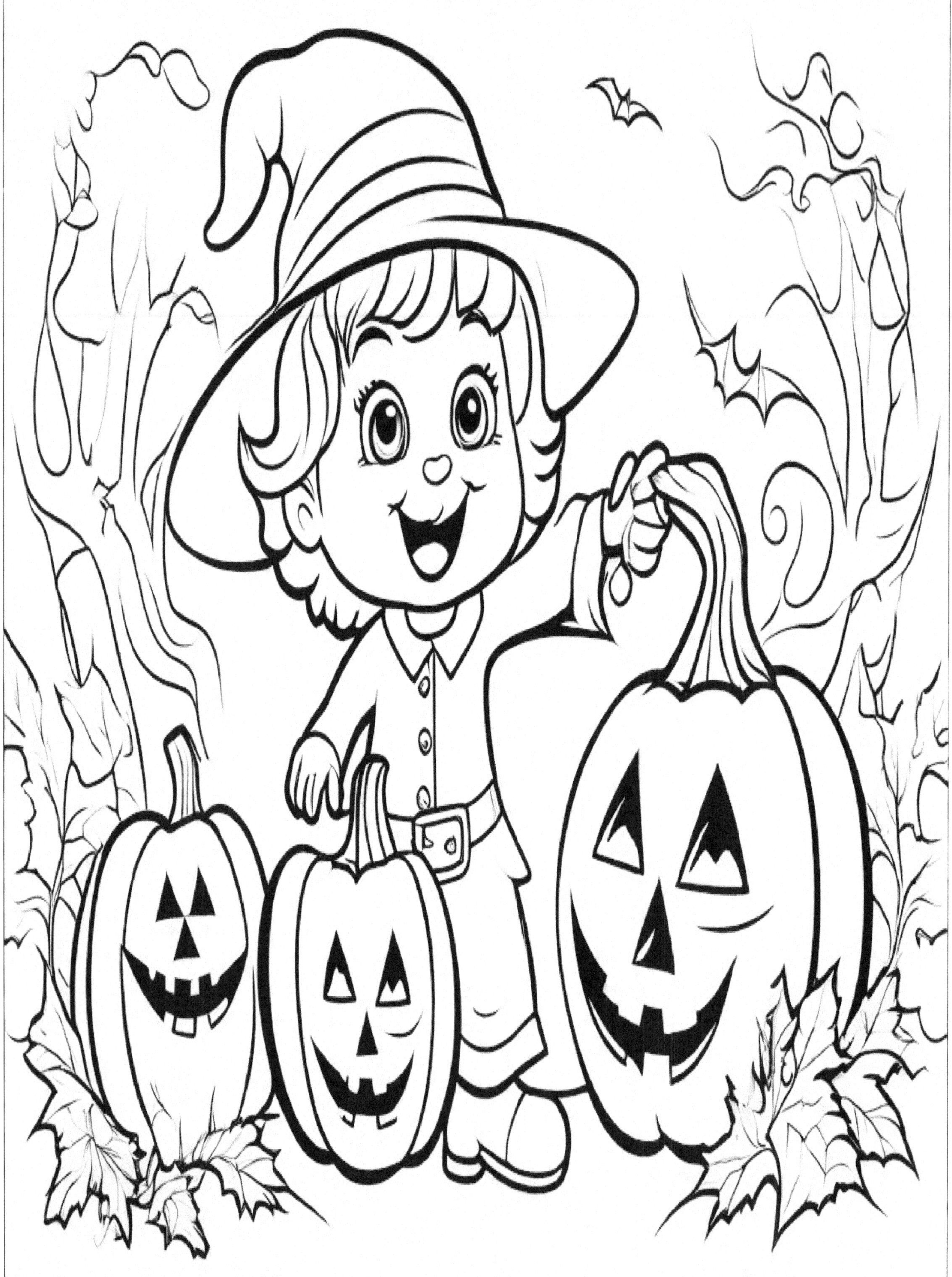

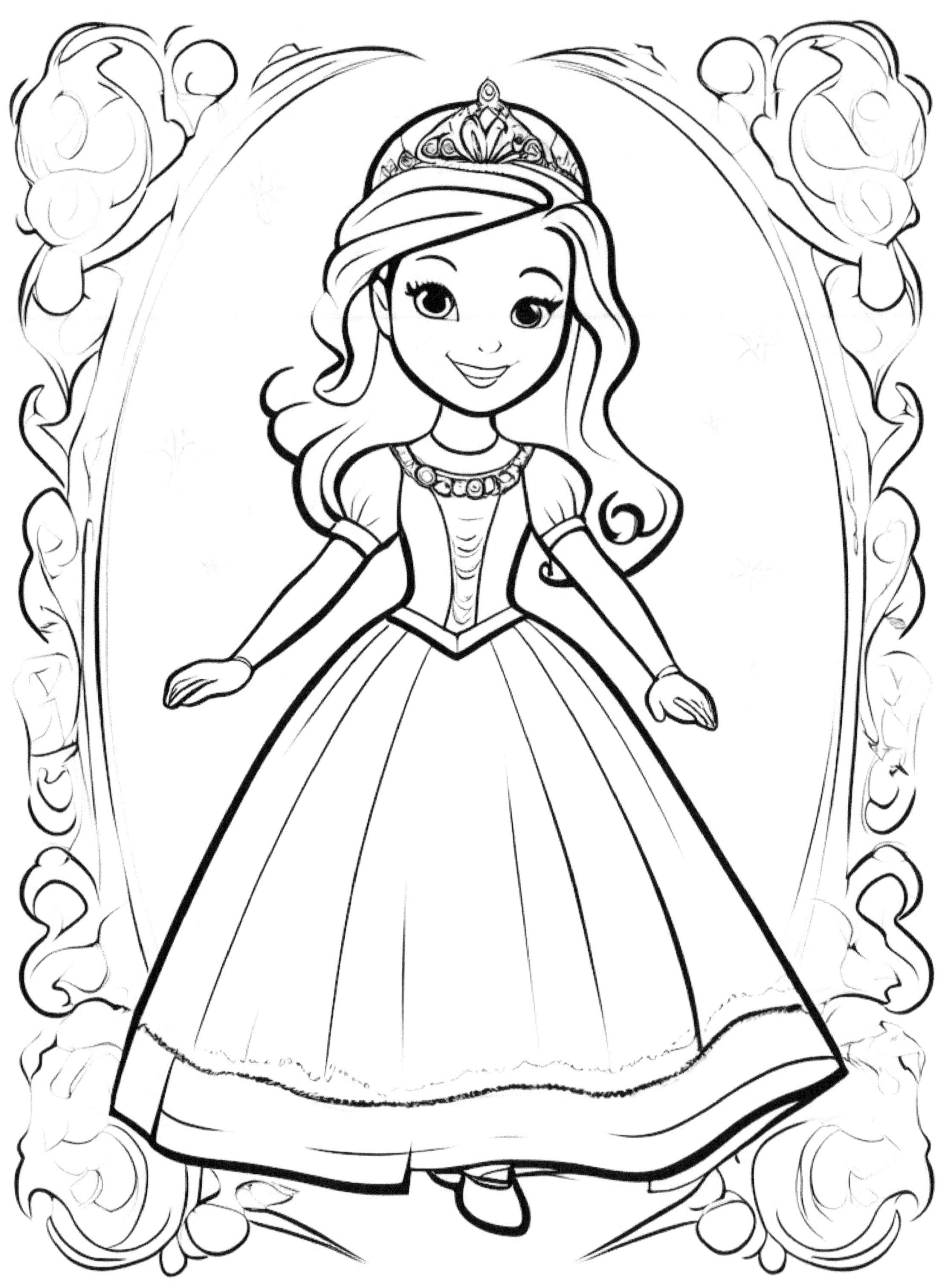

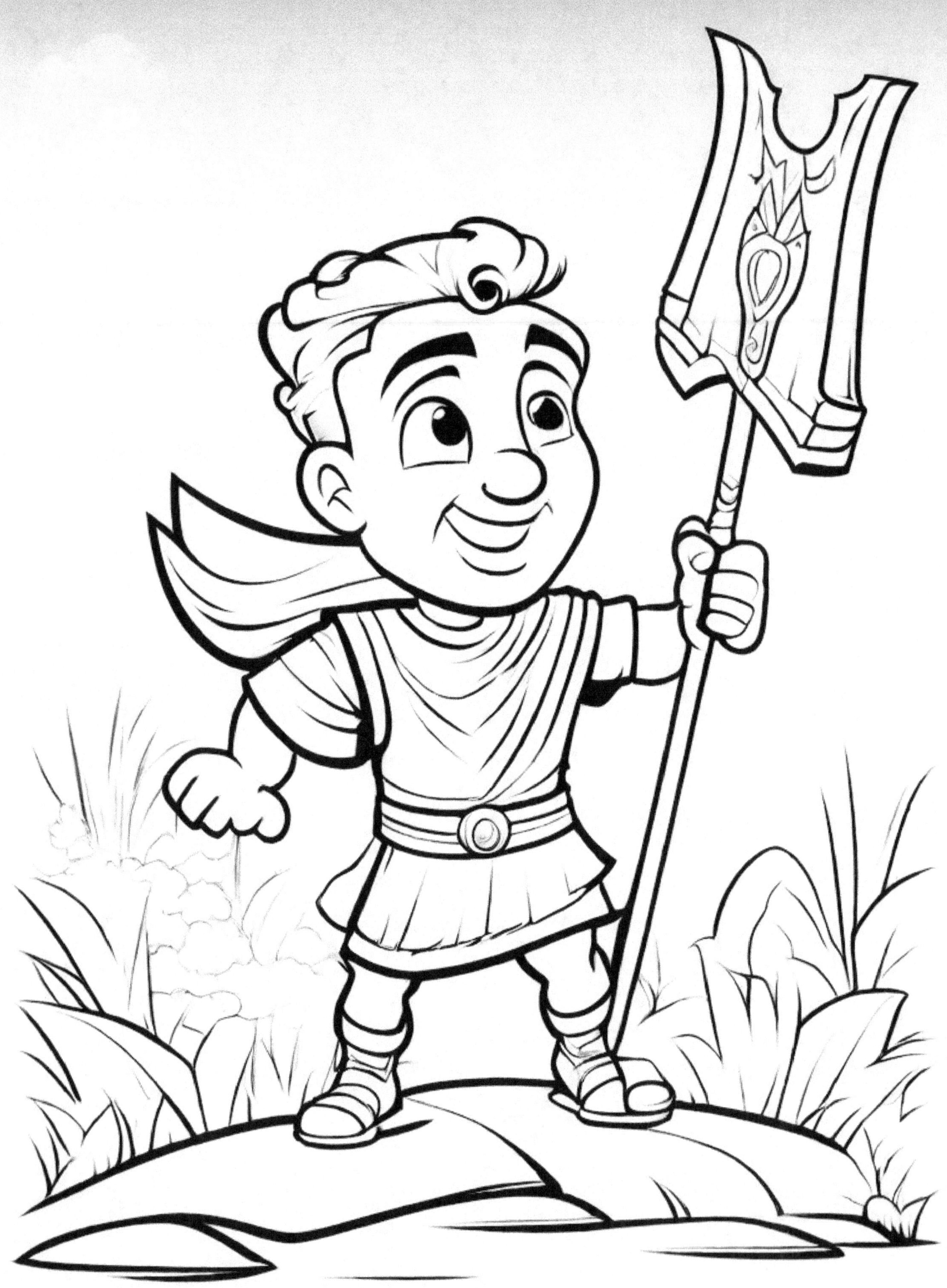

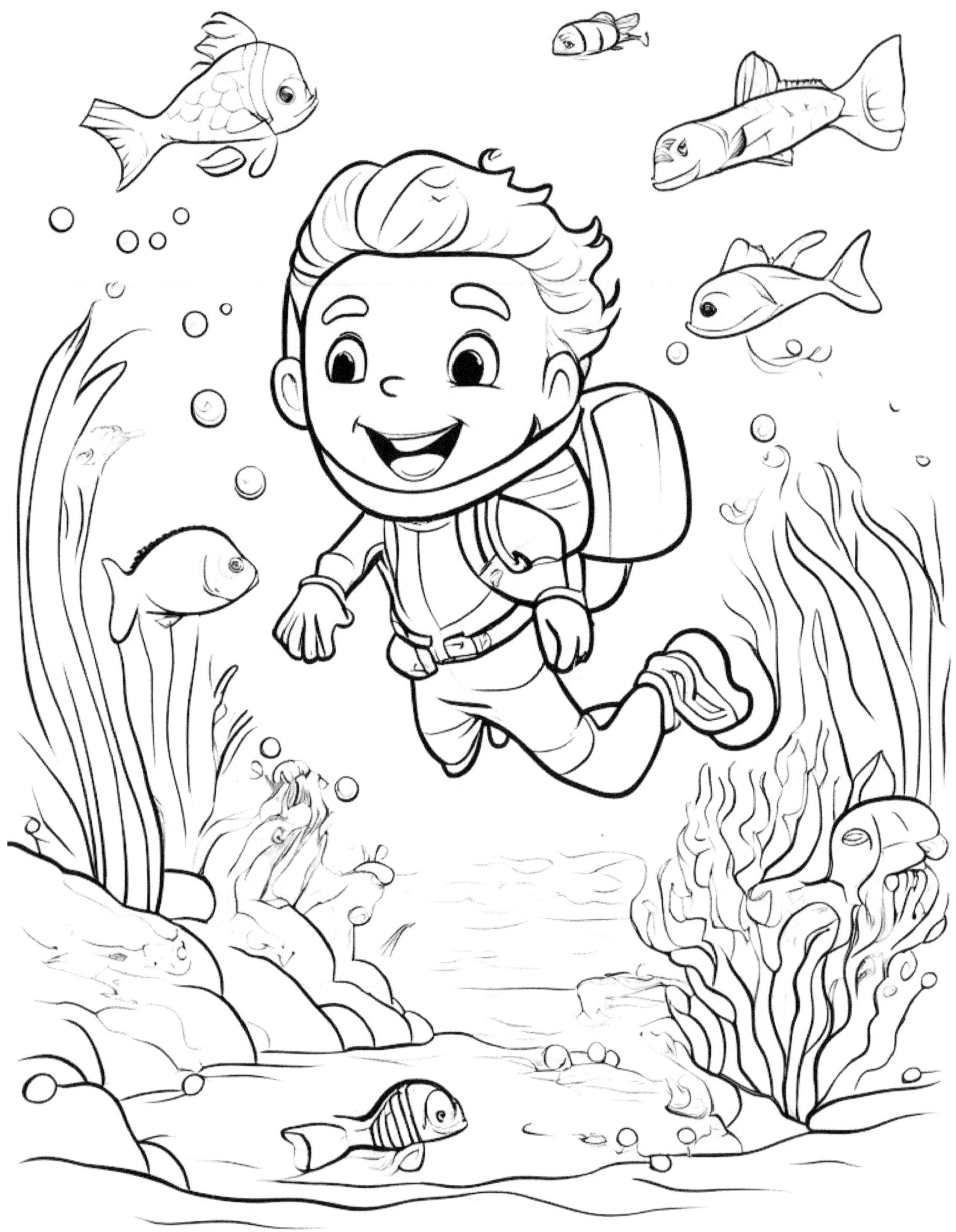

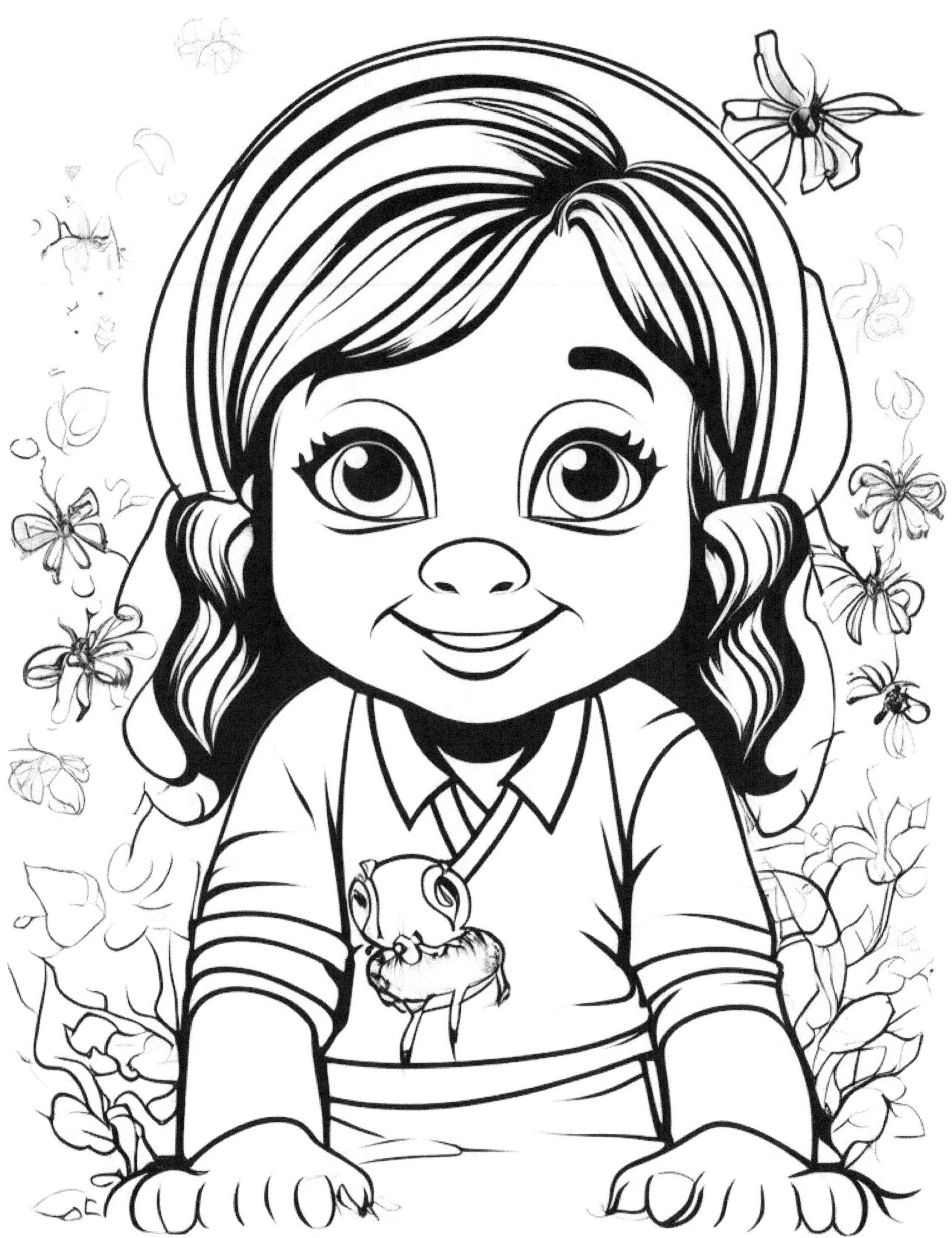

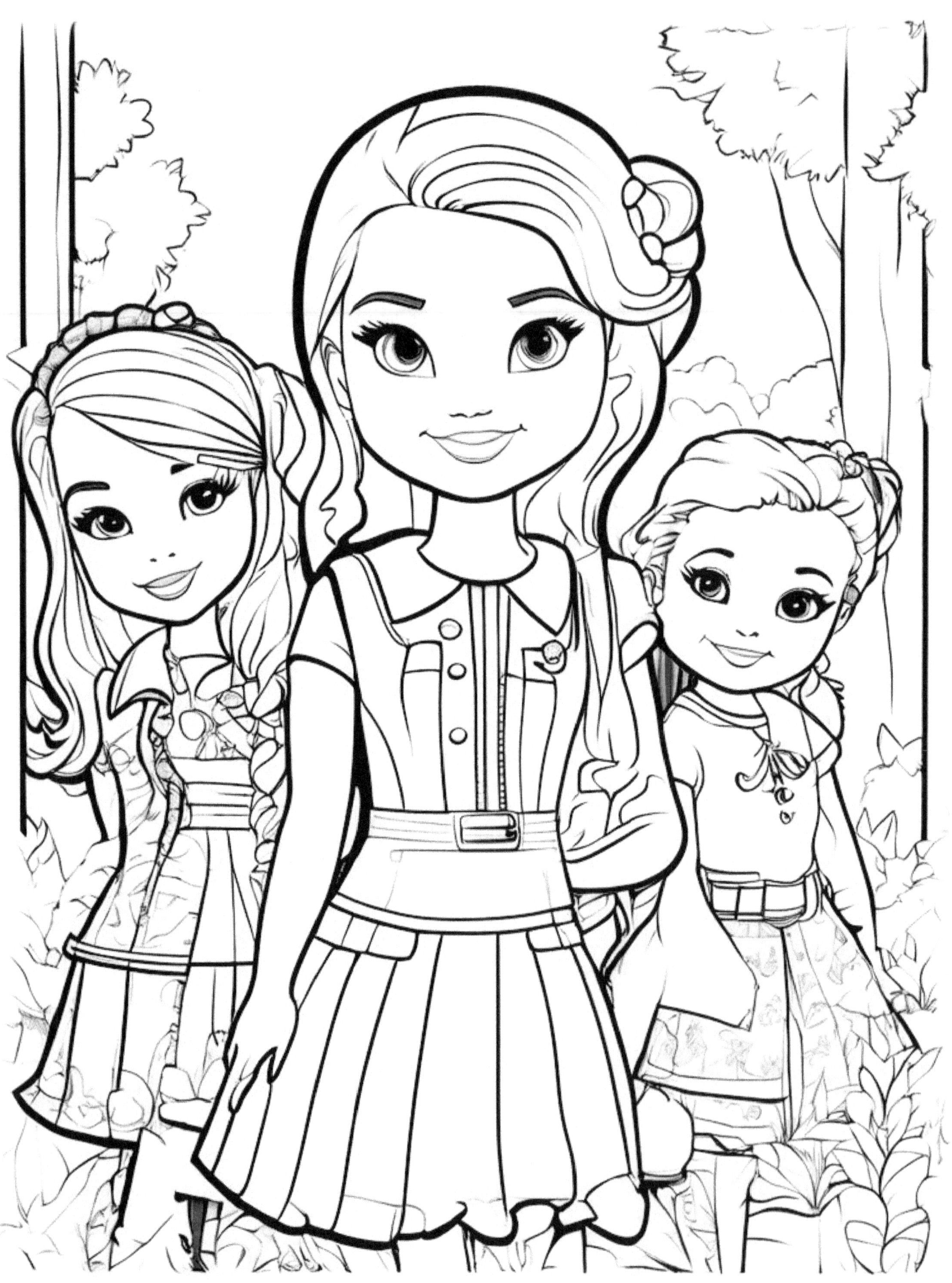

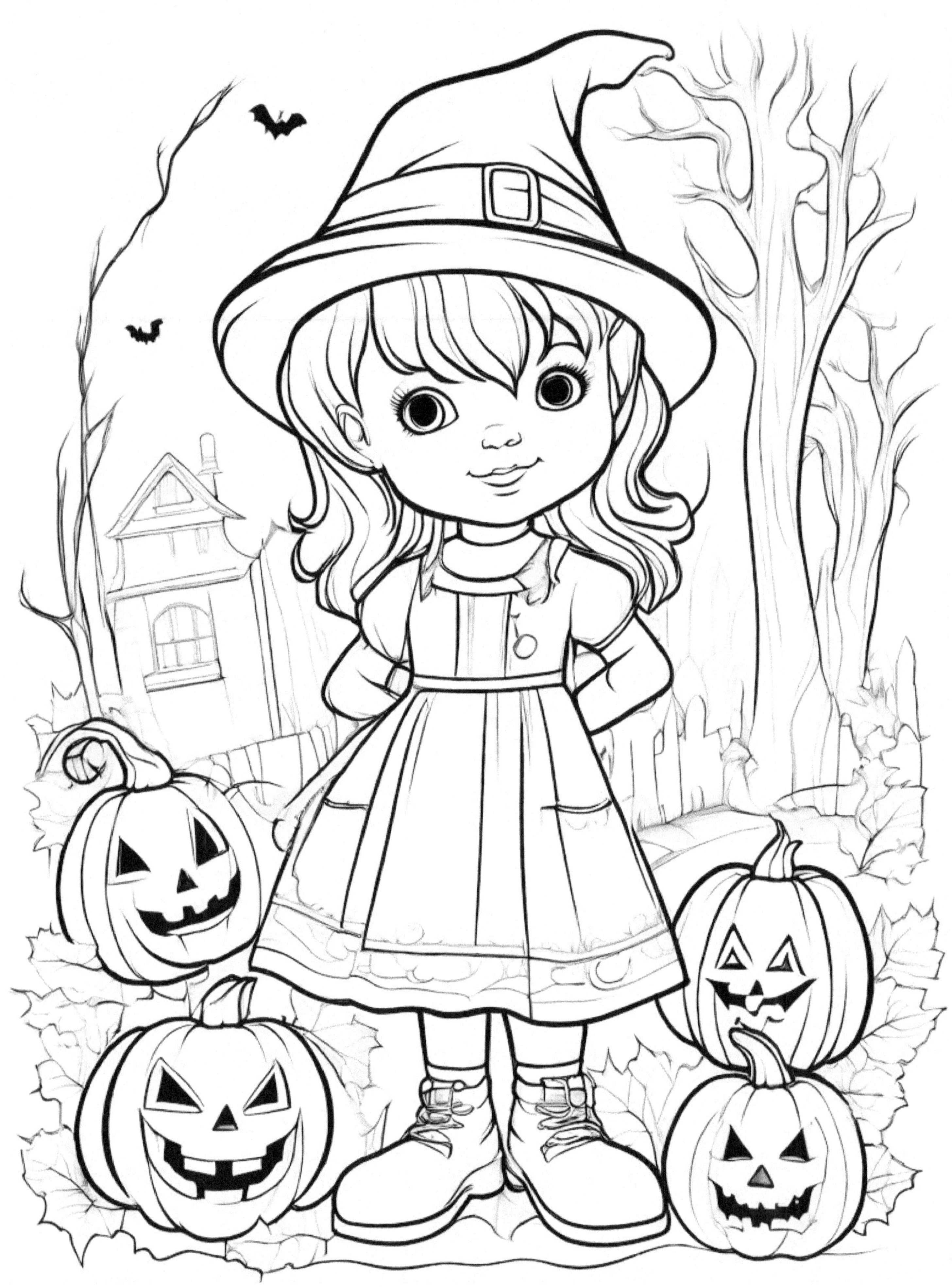

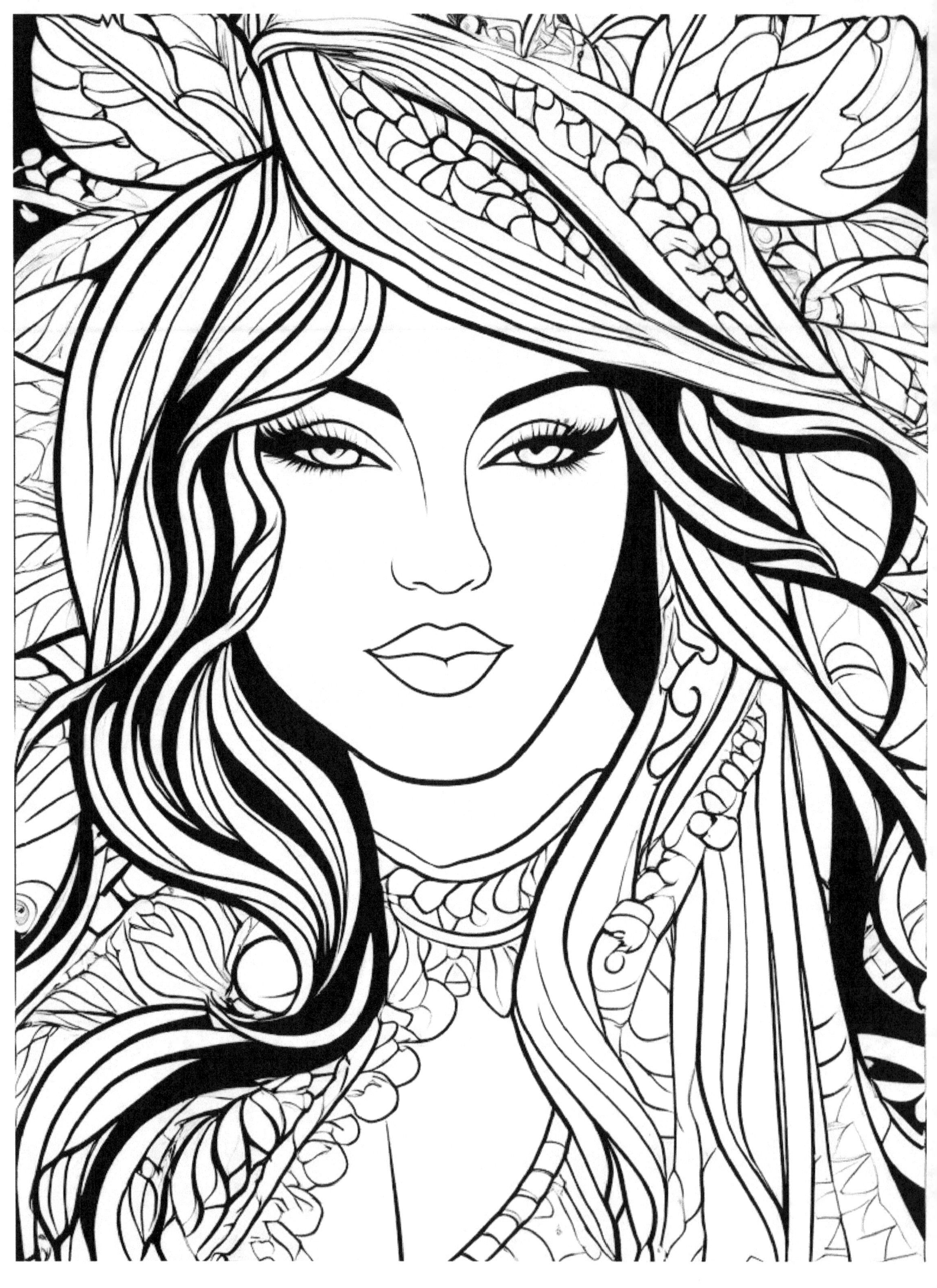

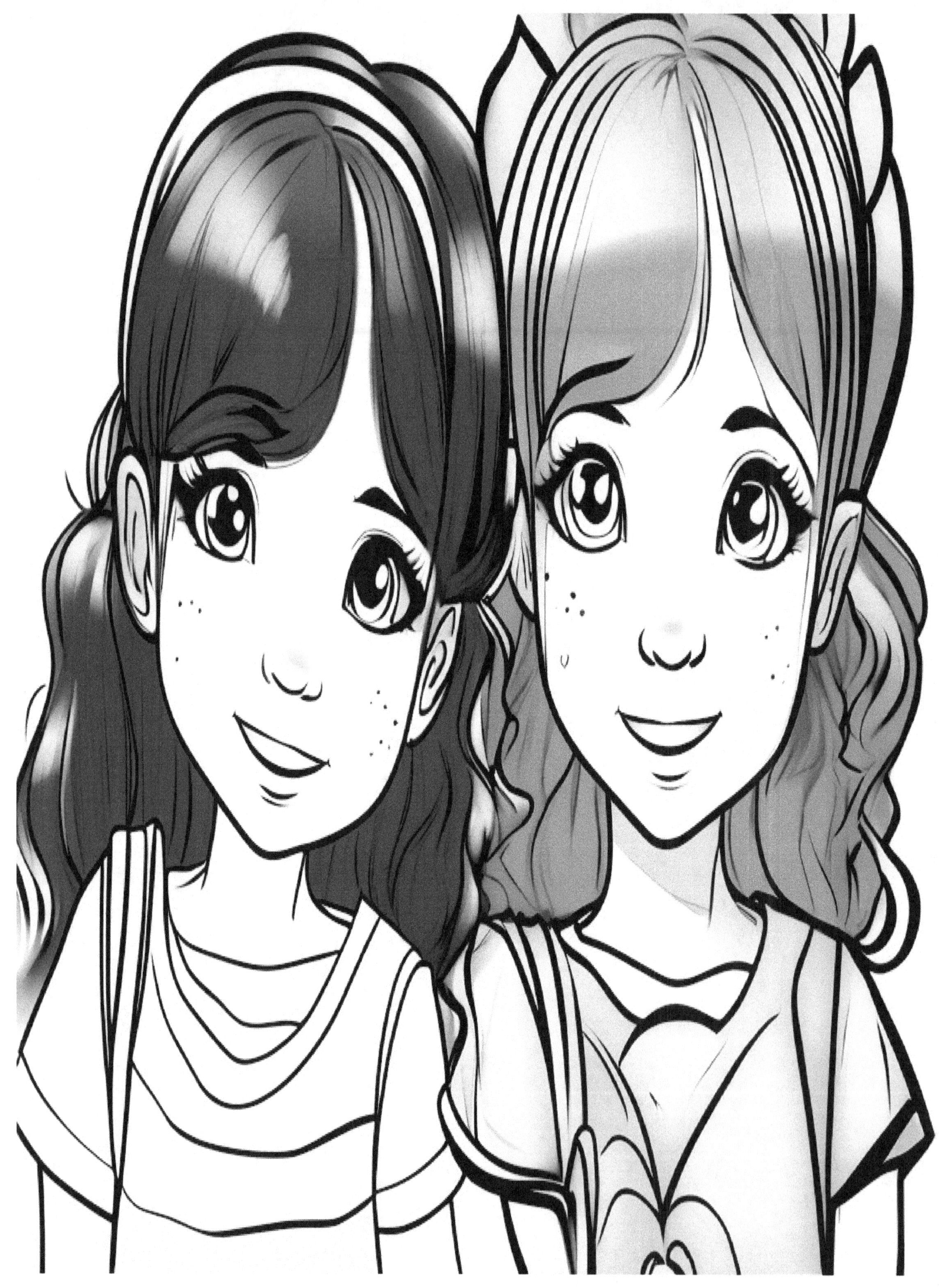

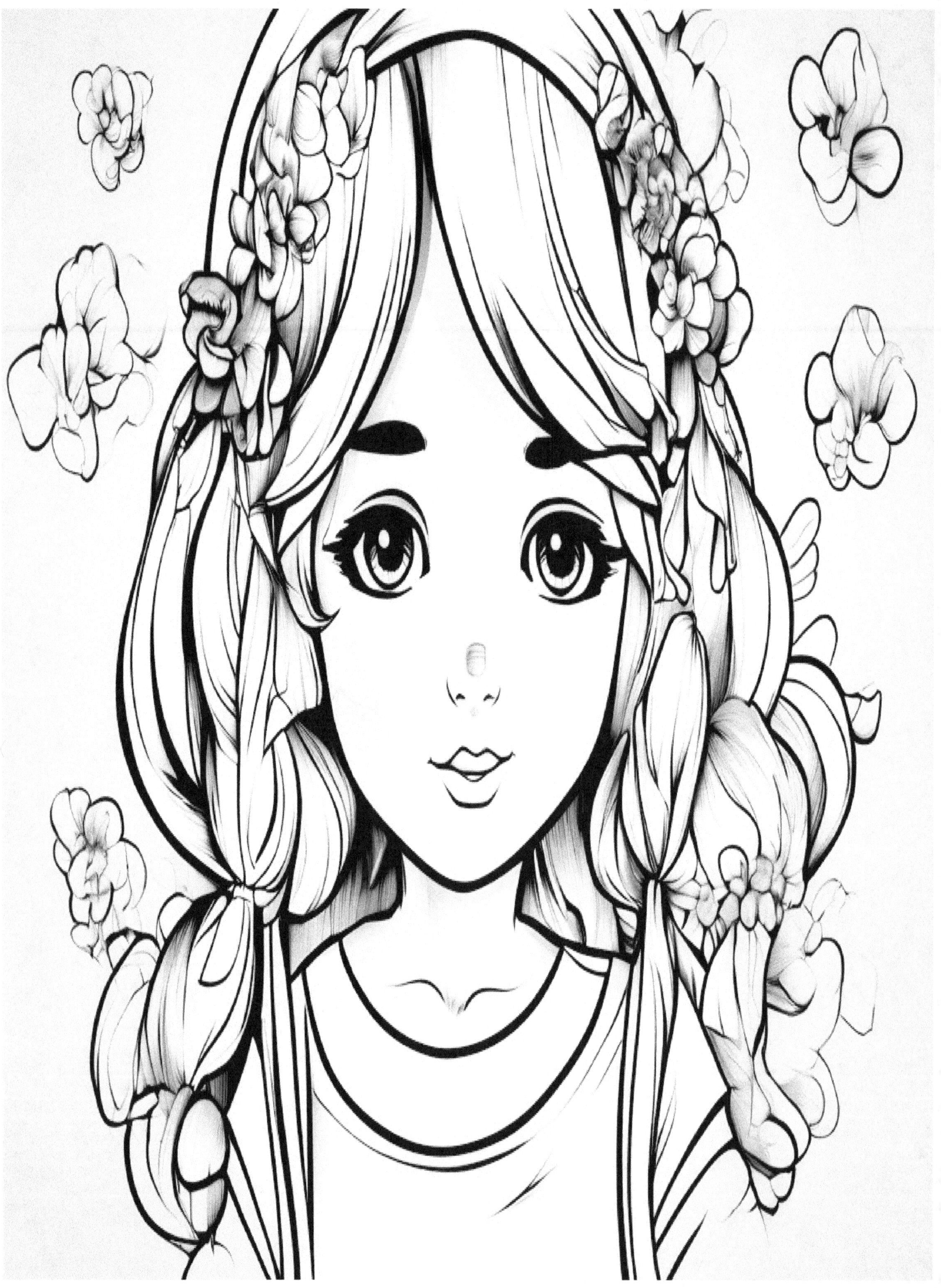

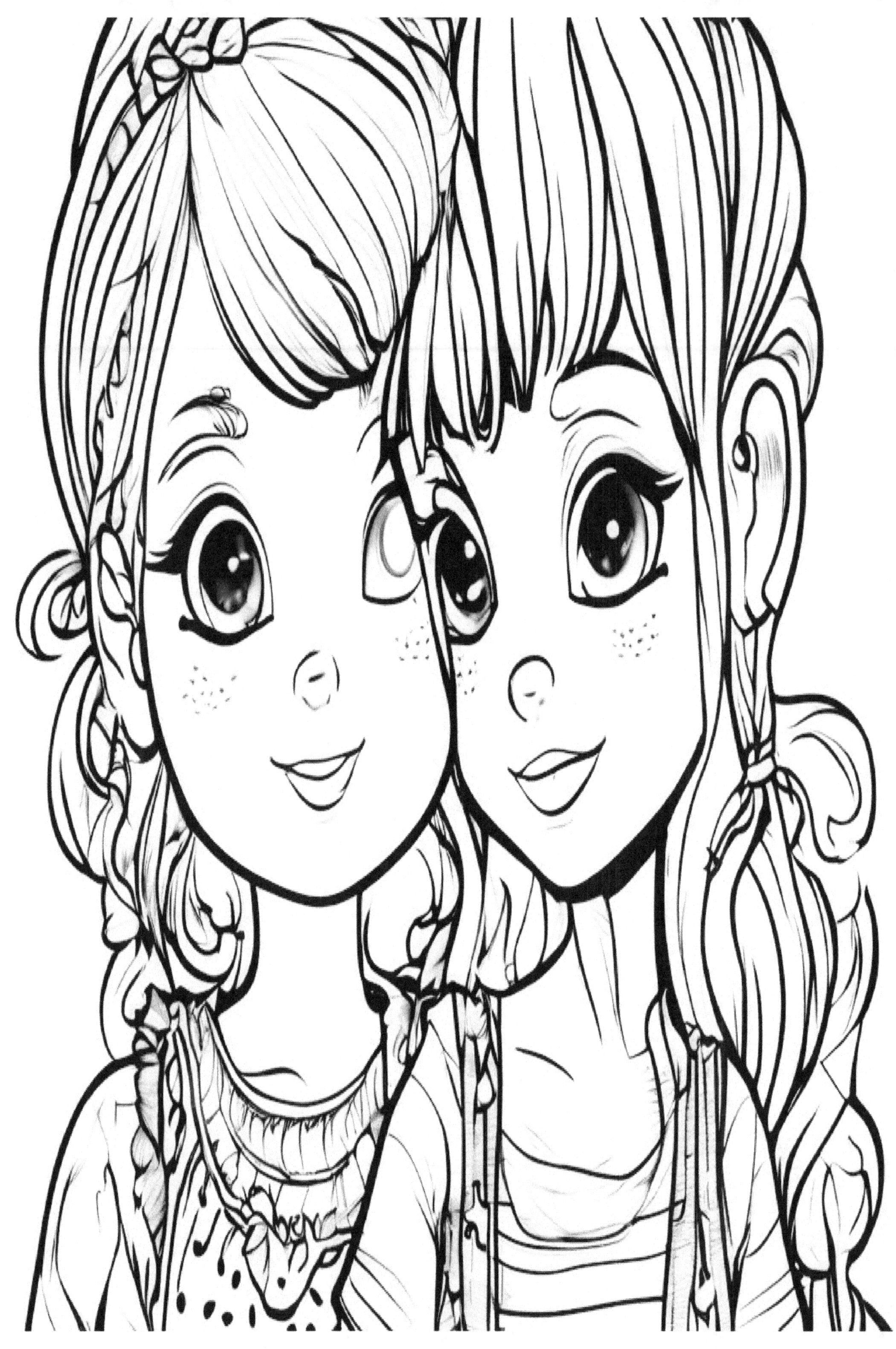

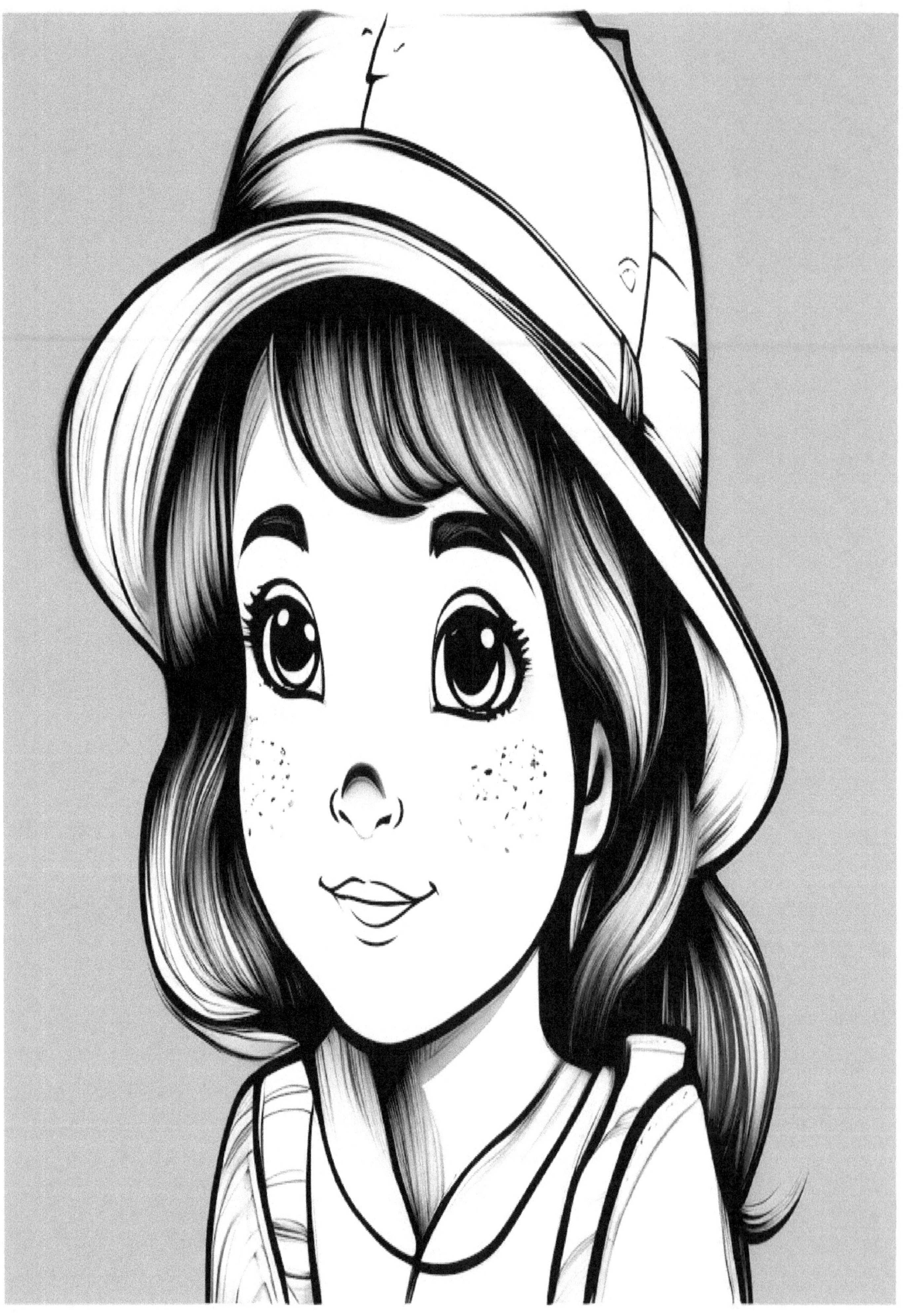

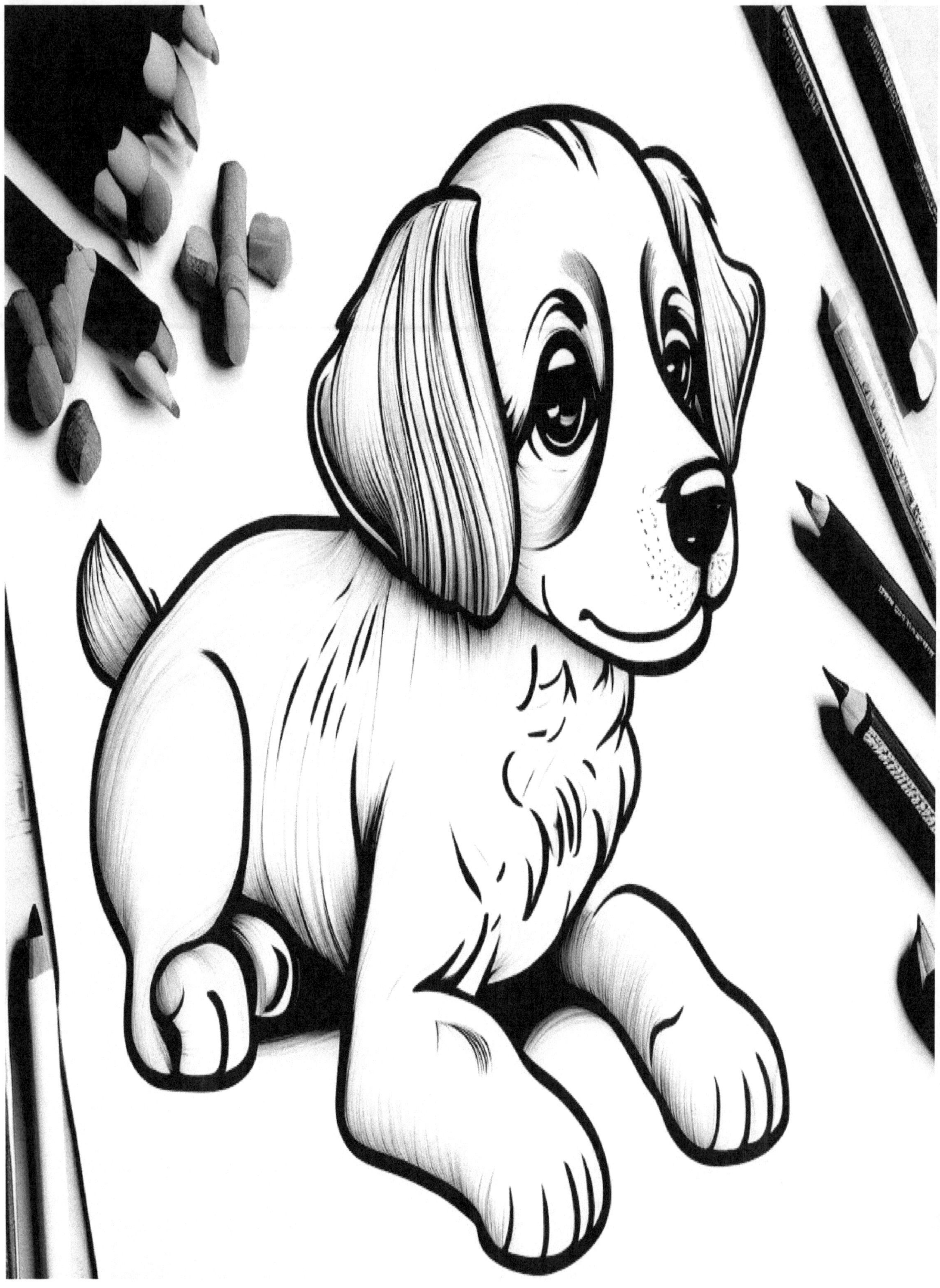

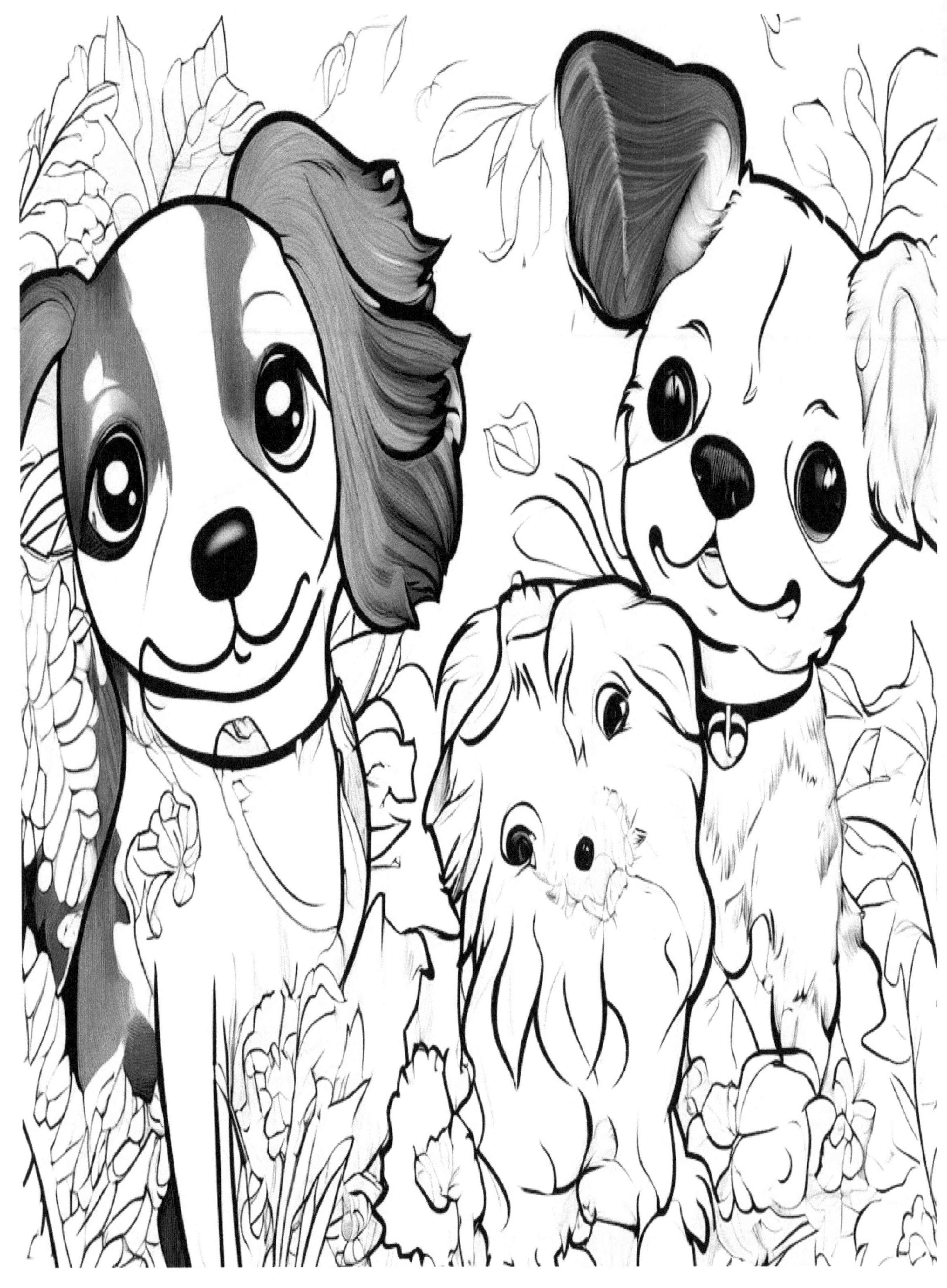

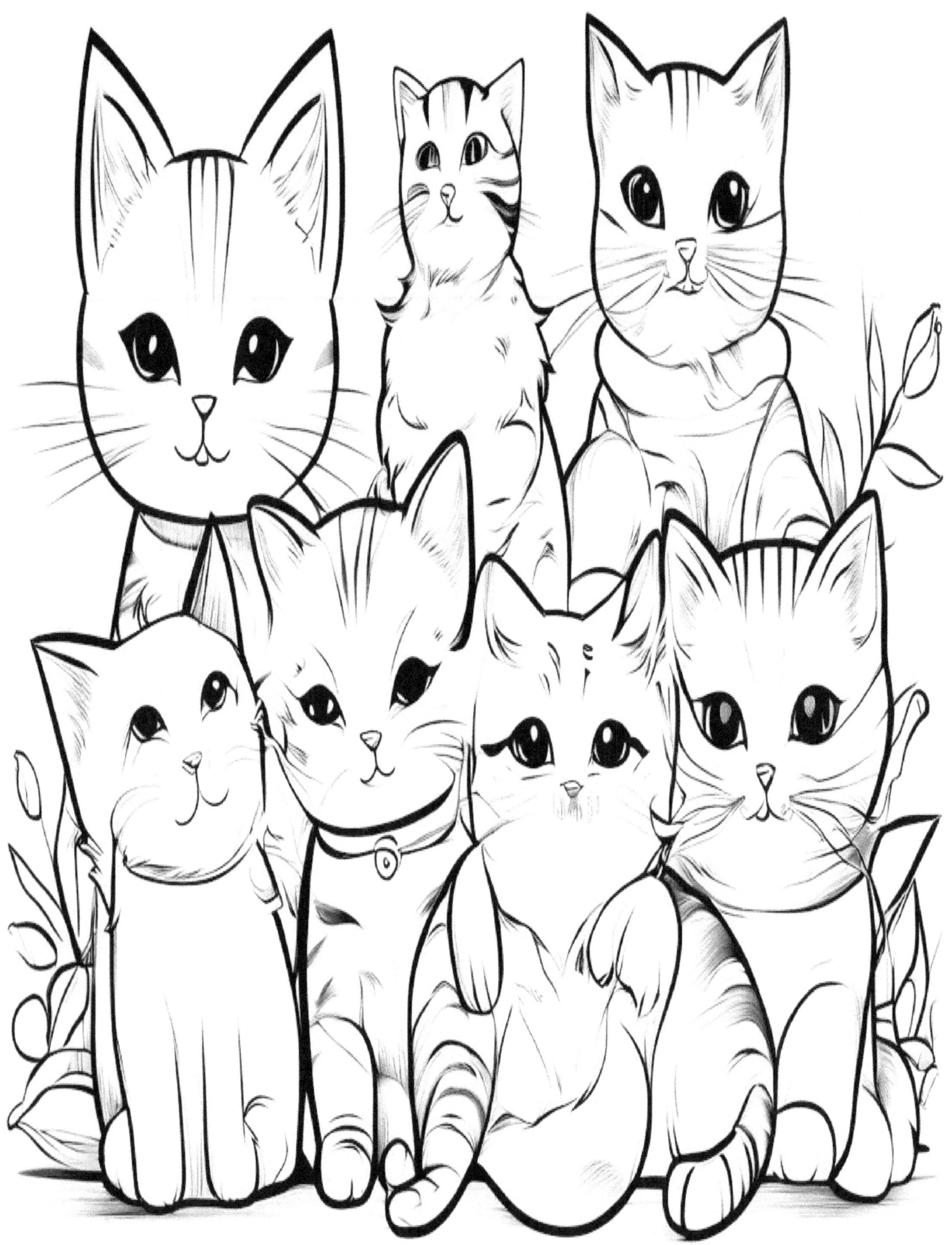

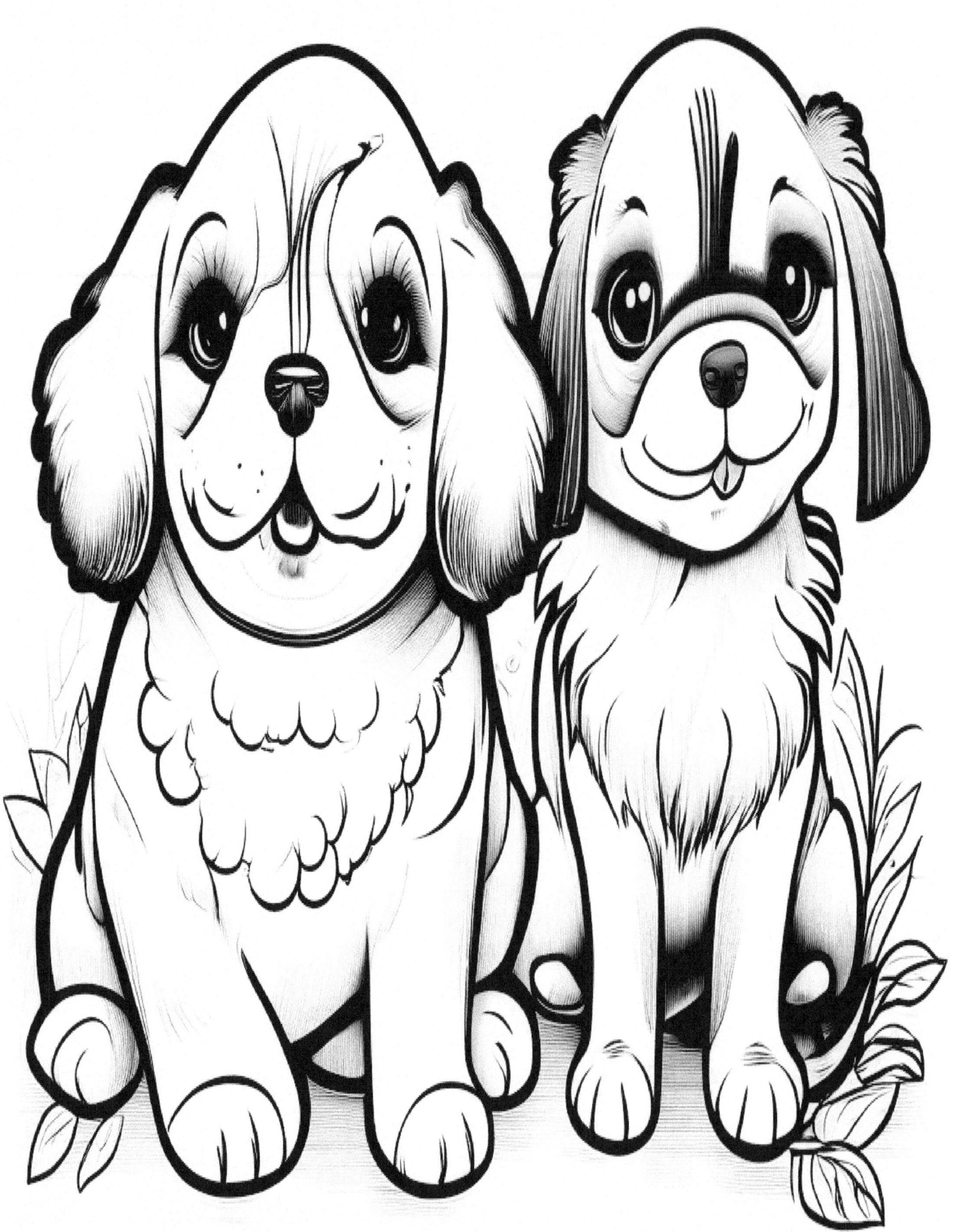

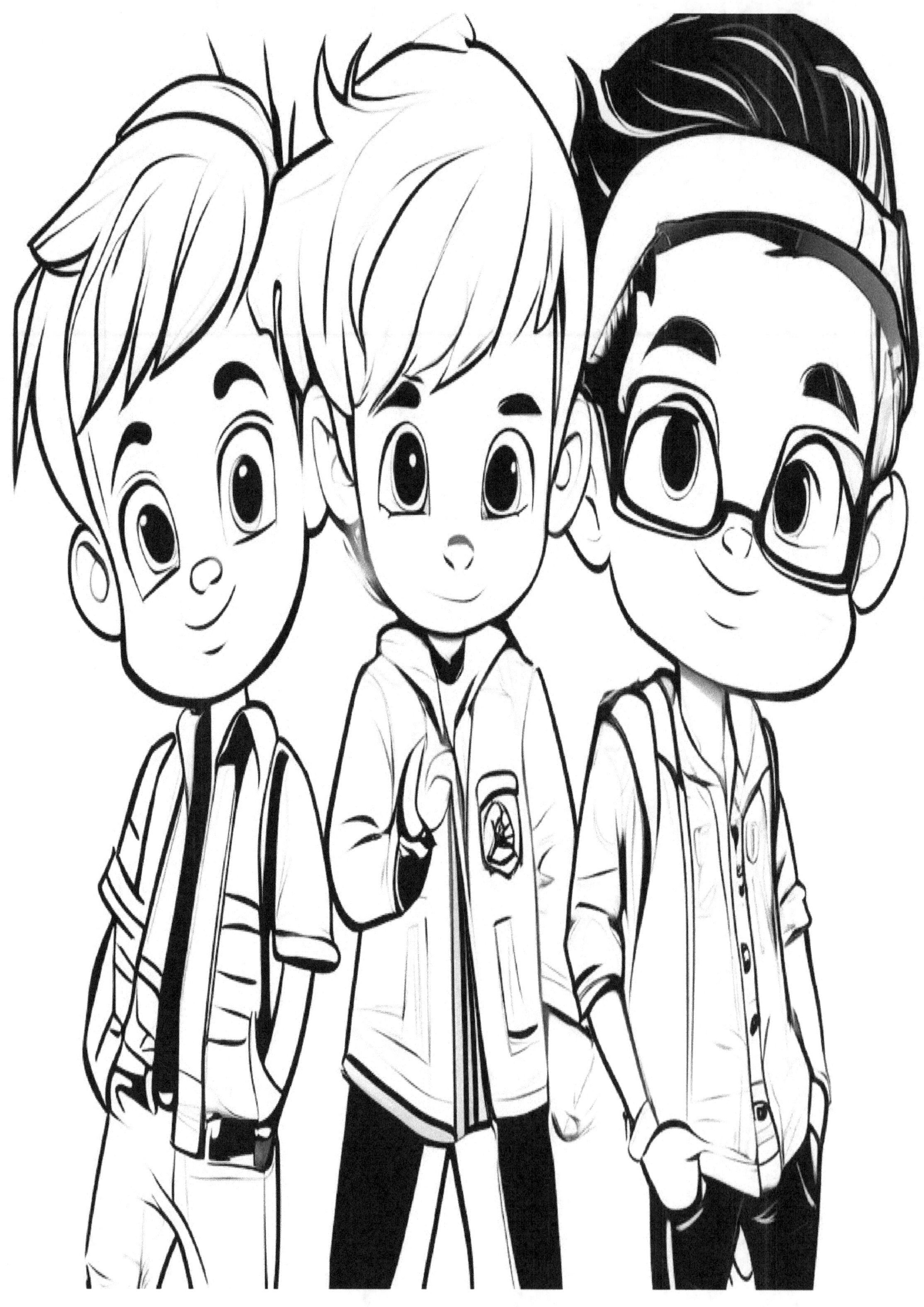

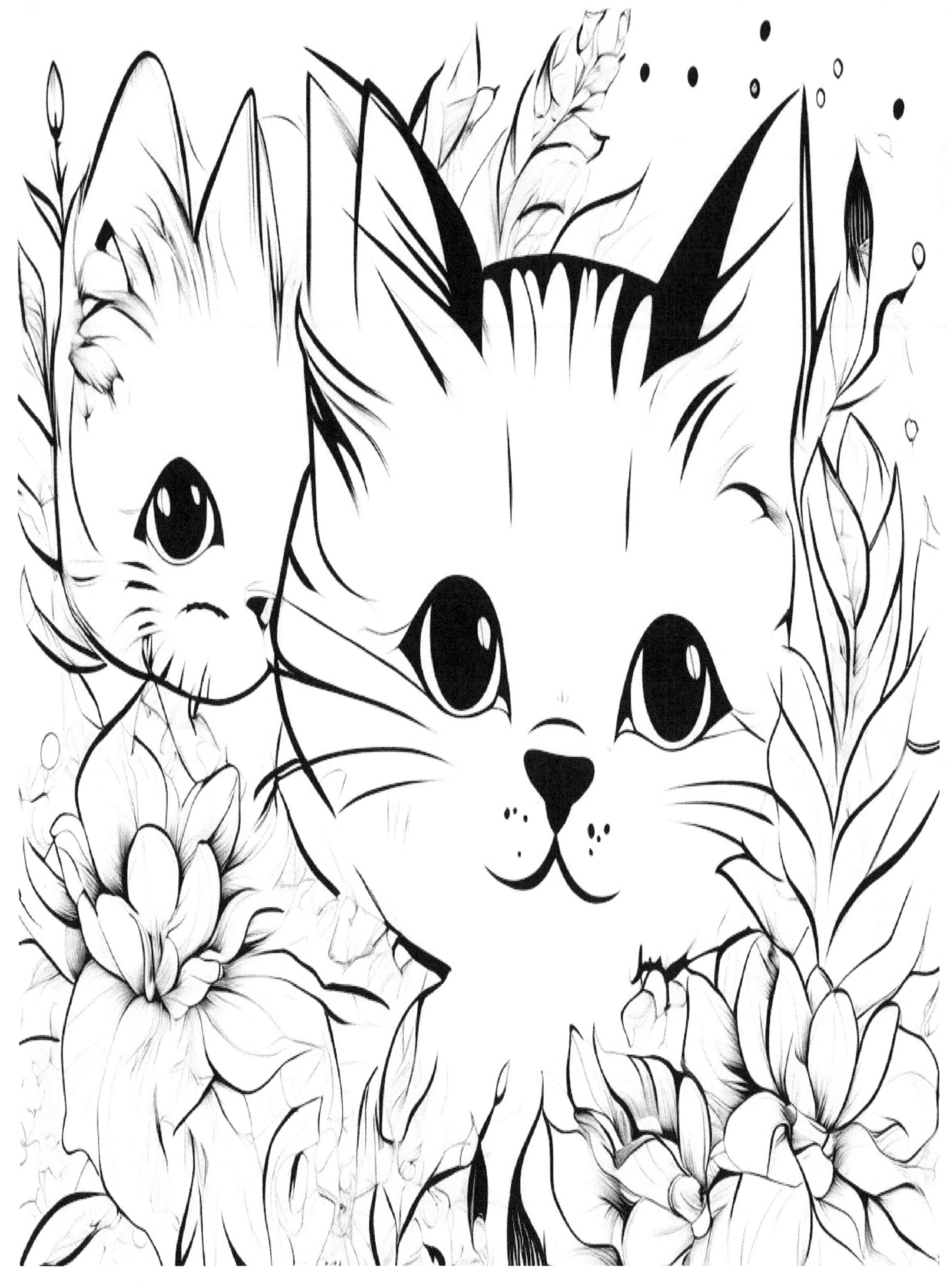

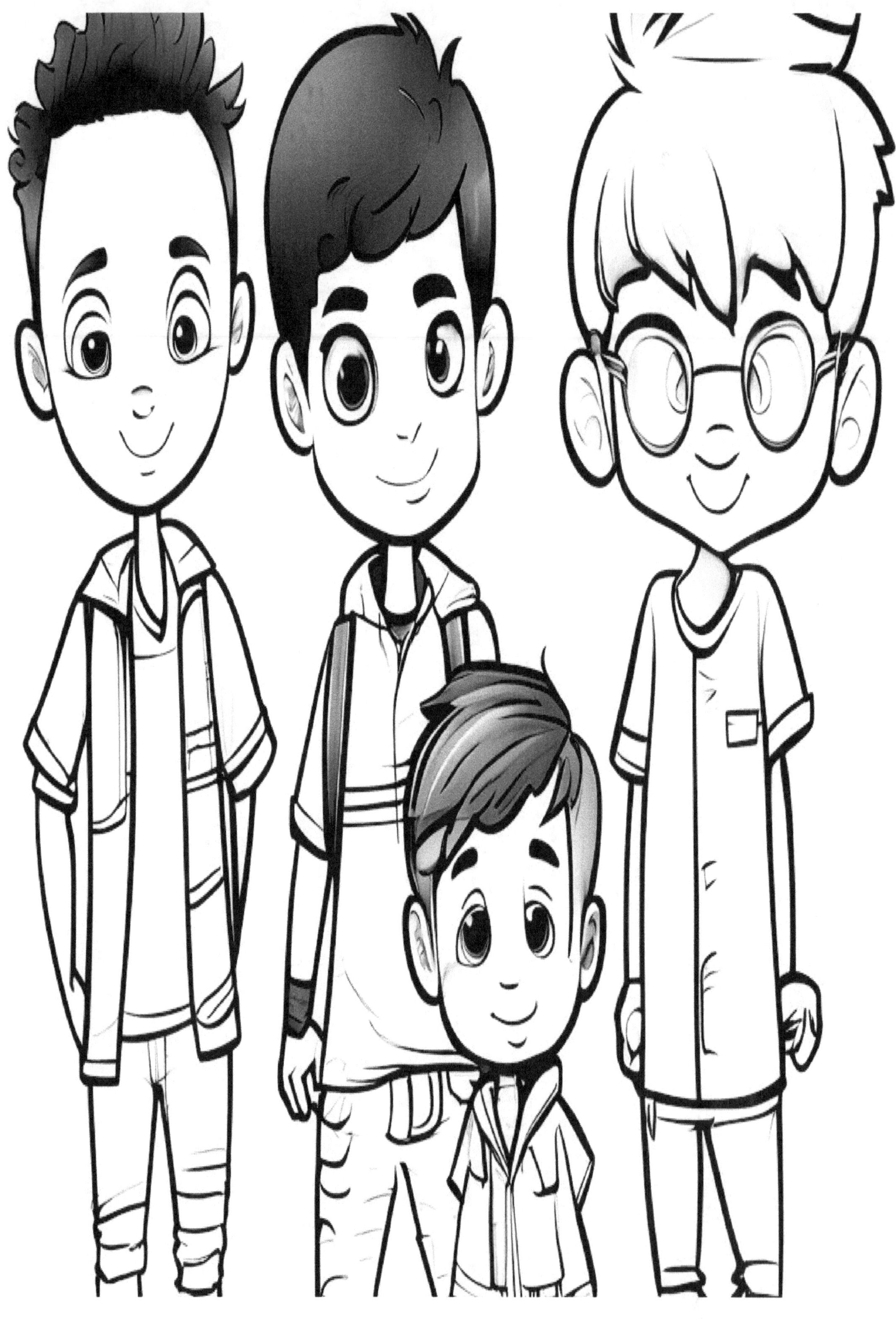

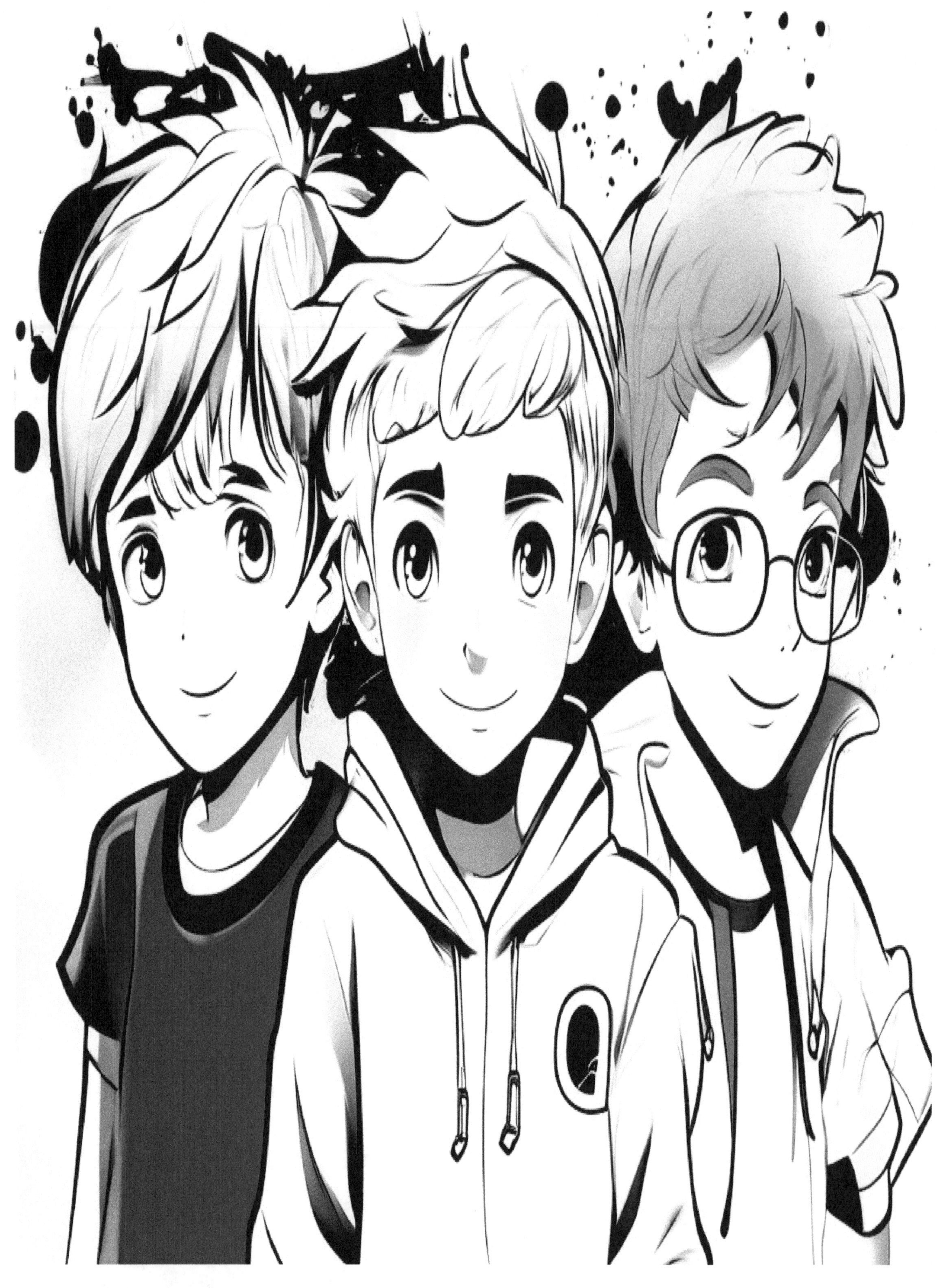

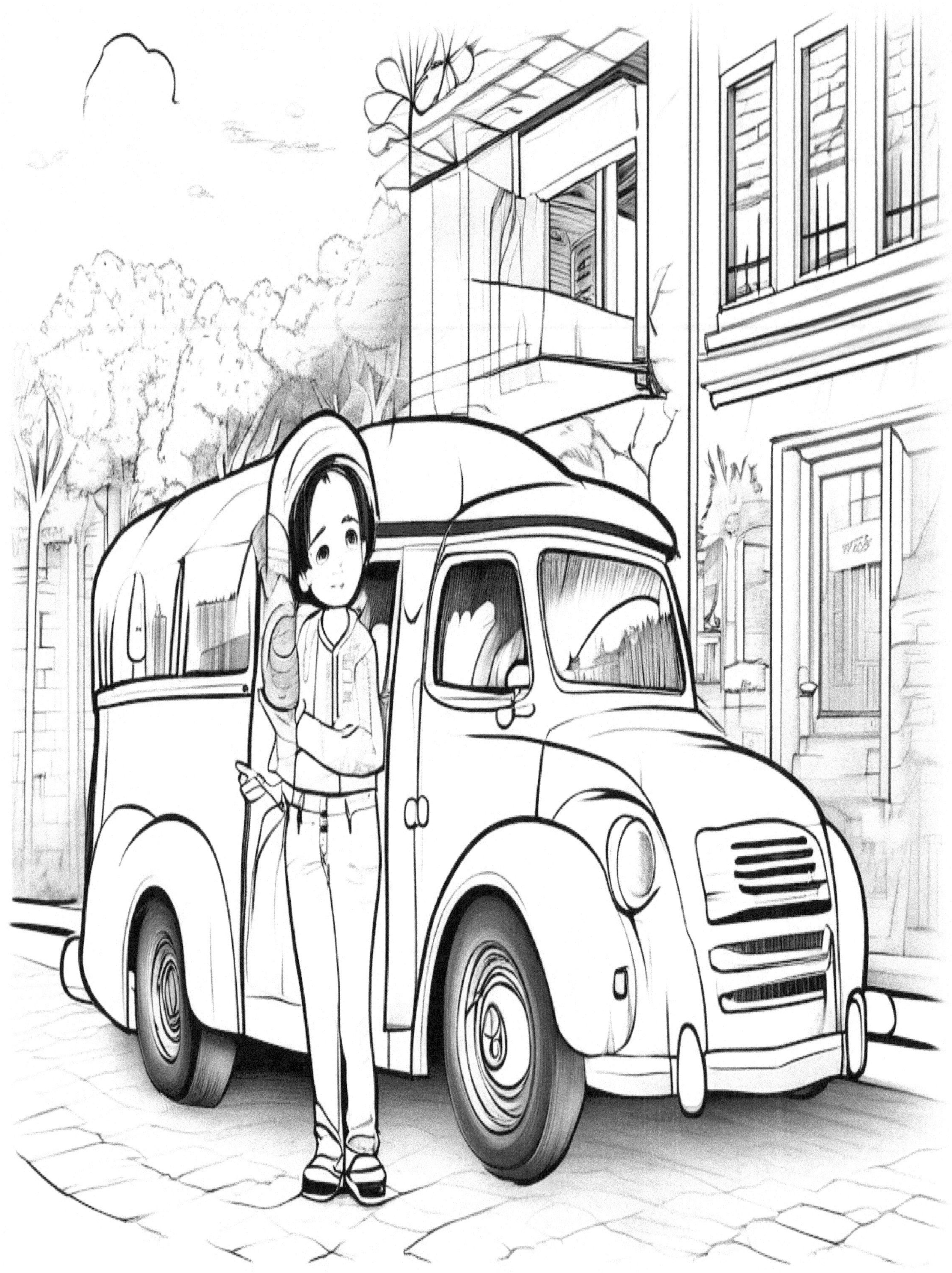

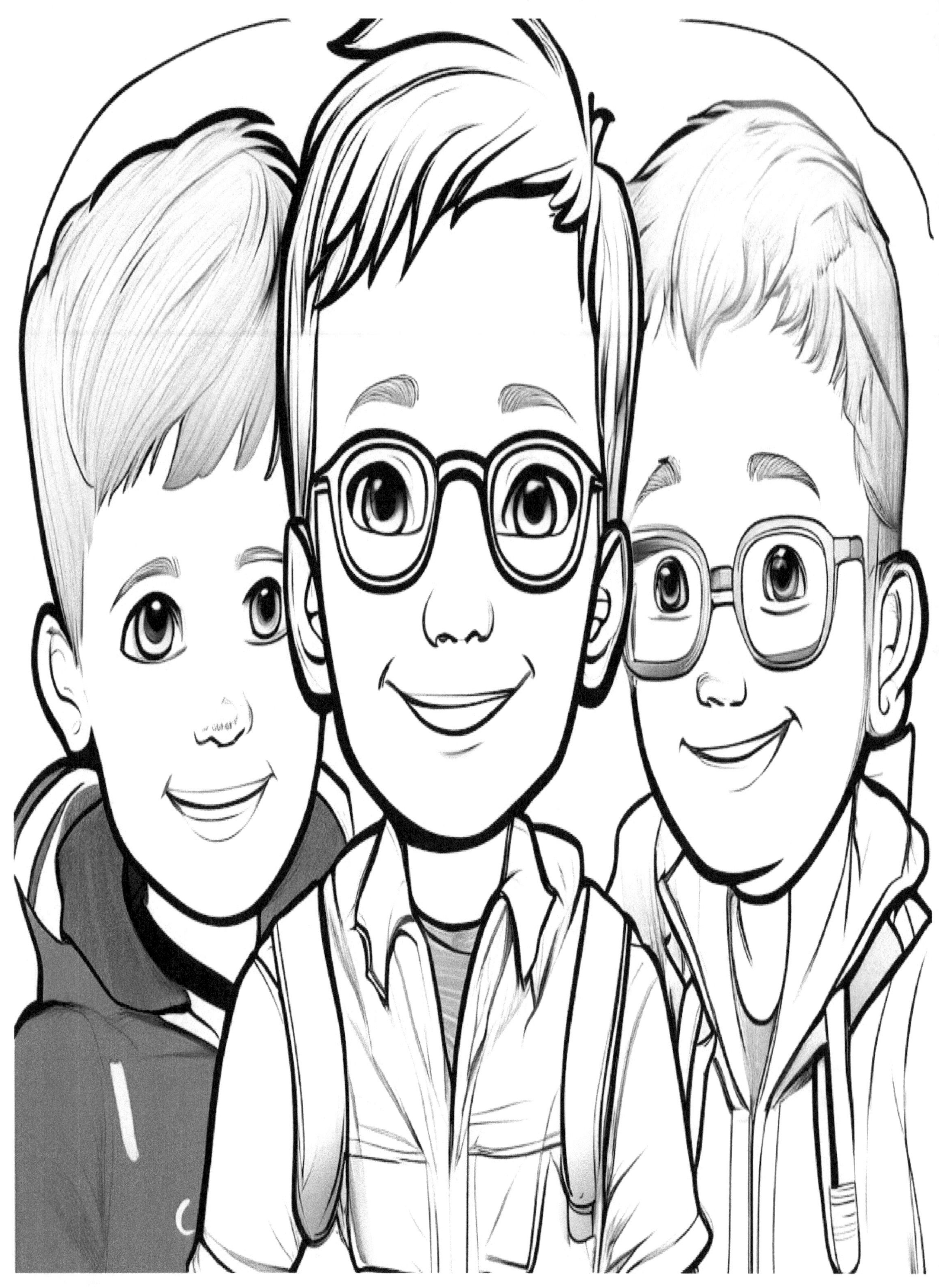

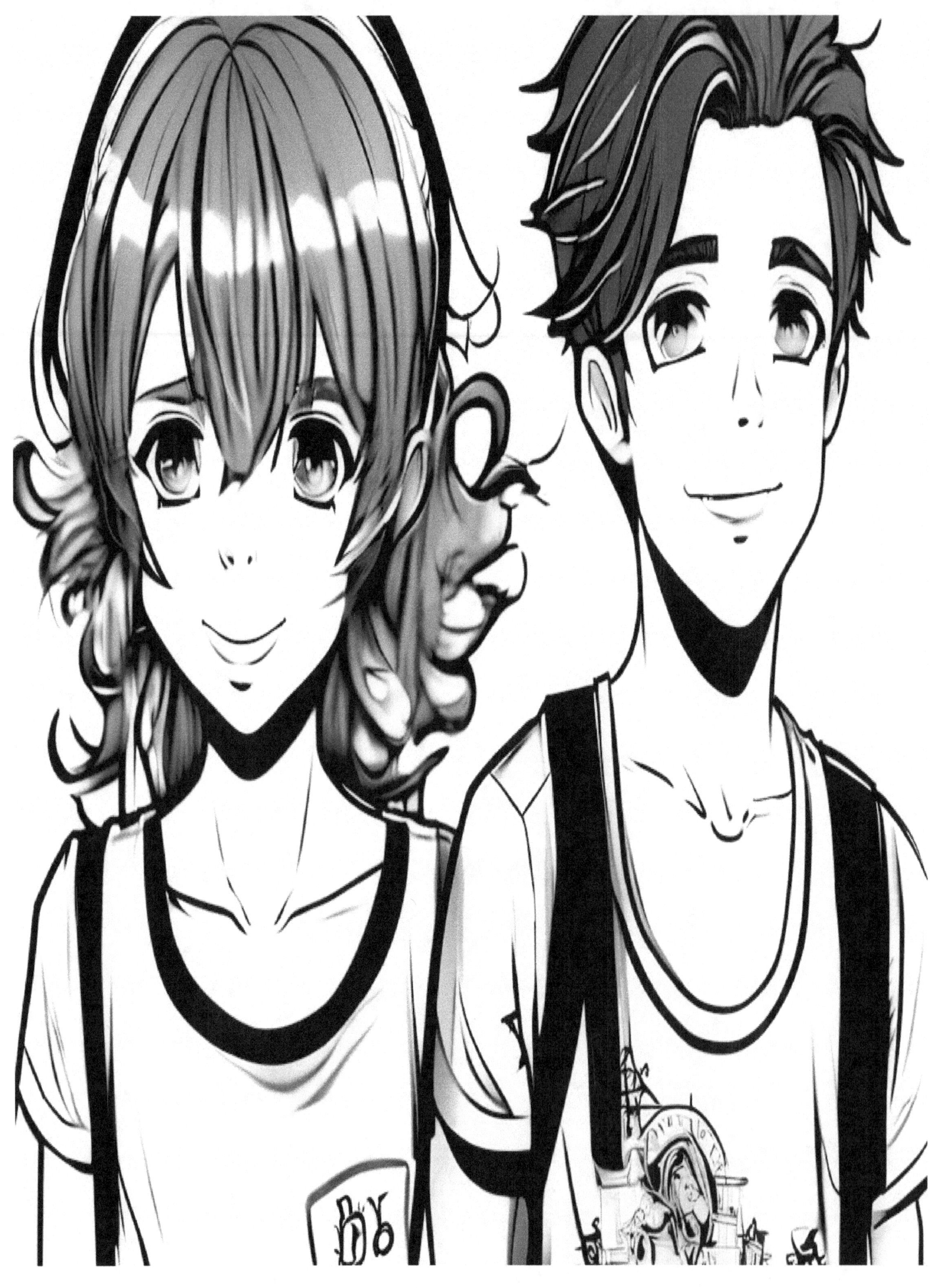

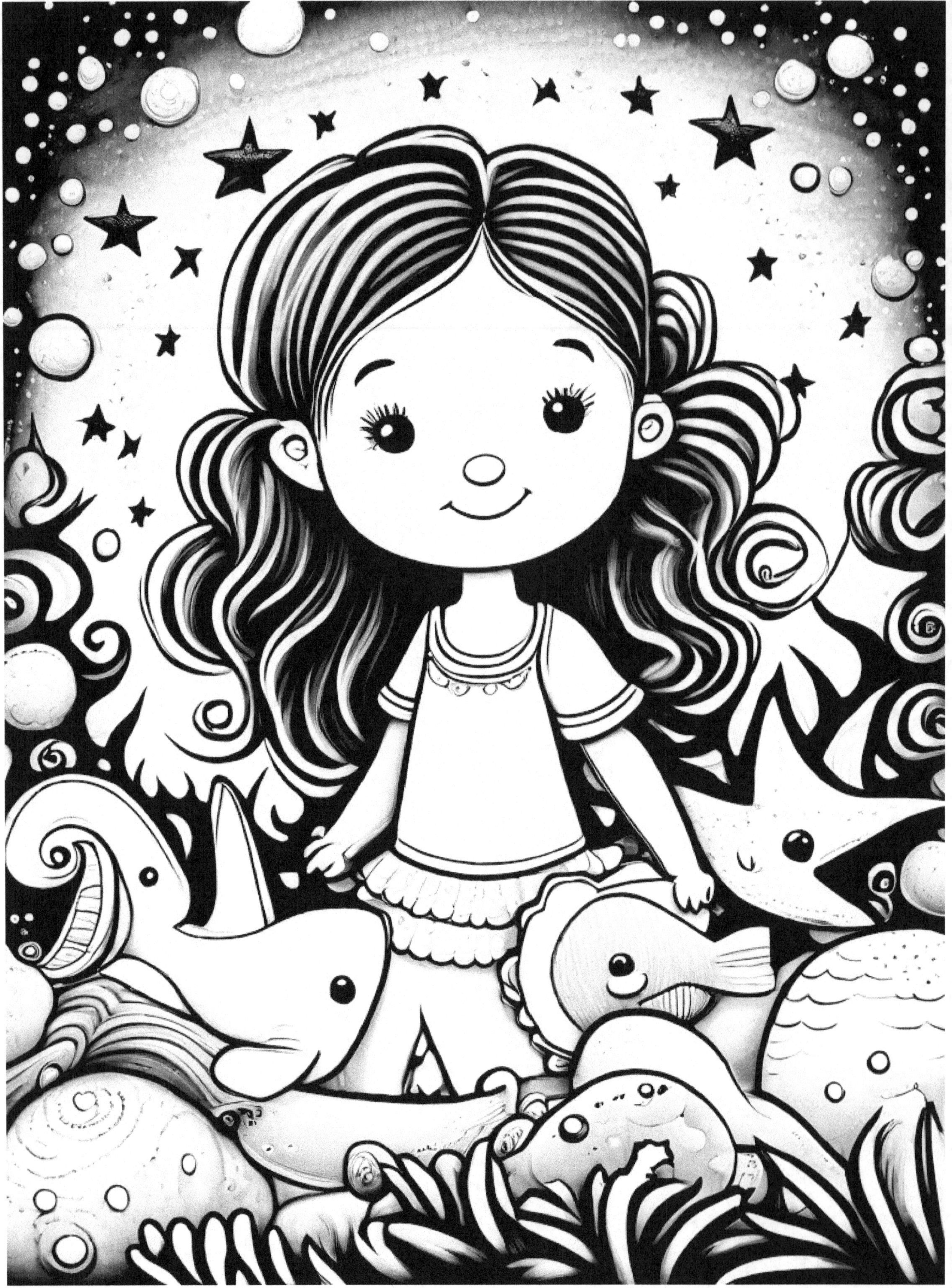

www.ingramcontent.com/pod-product-compliance
Lightning Source LLC
Chambersburg PA
CBHW082342270726
48658CB00017B/2962